TAKE A SWING AT
HITTING FOR THE CIRCUIT

He's the only player ever to smack three homers in a game in his final season. Single.

Who were the first keystone pair to both win Gold Gloves in the same year? Two bases, plus an RBI for the year.

The Cubs got Doug Clemens and two former 20-game winners for Lou Brock. The pair of ex-20-gamers won a grand total of seven victories in Bruin garb. Name 'em for a triple.

In 1937, he came within a single point of the NL record at his position when he fielded .986. No NL'er since has come so close to the circuit's all-time top mark. He rates a homer, but take a sac hit if you know only the position he played.

Okay. All warmed up? Then turn the page to start playing the best game of your baseball life!

THE
BASEBALL CHALLENGE
QUIZ BOOK

The Baseball Challenge Quiz Book

by

David Nemec

A SIGNET BOOK

SIGNET
Published by the Penguin Group
Penguin Books USA Inc., 375 Hudson Street,
New York, New York 10014, U.S.A.
Penguin Books Ltd, 27 Wrights Lane,
London W8 5TZ, England
Penguin Books Australia Ltd, Ringwood,
Victoria, Australia
Penguin Books Canada Ltd, 2801 John Street,
Markham, Ontario, Canada L3R 1B4
Penguin Books (N.Z.) Ltd, 182-190 Wairau Road,
Auckland 10, New Zealand

Penguin Books Ltd, Registered Offices:
Harmondsworth, Middlesex, England

First published by Signet, an imprint of New American Library,
a division of Penguin Books USA Inc.

First Printing, April, 1991
10 9 8 7 6 5 4 3 2 1

CONTENTS

JUNE

JULY

AUGUST

SEPTEMBER

OCTOBER

INTRODUCTION

Ready . . . set . . . here we go again. The odds are that if you scored well in my previous quiz books, you'll do yourself equally proud this trip. All the names and events you'll encounter in these pages should once more strike a familiar chord, and hence there'll be very few questions that you can shrug off as being impossible for all but a superexpert.

Sounds as if you ought to have an easy enough time, doesn't it? And you will, provided you have the wherewithal to puzzle out answers that you don't necessarily have on the tip of your tongue. That's the real acid test. That's what finally distinguishes the superstars of baseball memorabilia. Not computer memories but a talent for sitting down with a few clues, a couple of disparate facts or stats, and making the correct connection between them.

Baseball. It eats up your brain. It is designed to eat up your brain. The game mesmerizes you early on with its simple pattern of three strikes, three outs, three times three innings, and yet there is a vast kinetic quality to it too, an ineffably romantic quality that in the end is what hooks you for life. You sense it without being able to put your finger on it, feel it scraping away at the very nerve of who we are and what we can be. For baseball, unlike football or basketball or indeed any of the other forms of entertainment that give us what passes for our cultural superstars, has a built-in allowance for us all. Size is important but not critical. Looks matter but not much. Age counts but the Roses and the Niekros and the Wilhelms somehow still find ways to stop time. Baseball at every moment in its history has been filled with performers whom all of us can fantasize we might have been had we just managed to stay in better shape and worked a little harder on our bunting and realized the importance a little sooner in life of learning to hit the cutoff man with our throws. There is a need certainly for raw talent, but there is a deeper quality aspect involved—the ever so slim line between success and failure in an endeavor that seems one of physical skill but at bottom is probably more a psychological test. How did a Nellie Fox make it and a Billy Consolo or a Ted Kazanski fall short? What drove Don Zimmer to keep coming back from one crippling injury after another while Herb Score went down for the count? Why is Nolan Ryan a household name and Steve Dalkowski a footnote in trivia books? Who could have foreseen that Phil Niekro, the possessor of only 32 victories on his 30th birthday, would get it together to have a Hall of Fame career whereas Steve Barber, Chuck Estrada, Wally Bunker, and Mark Fidrych—all of them big winners before they were barely of drinking age—would combine to net fewer career victories than Niekro? Why Mike Schmidt and not Dave Roberts or Joe Charboneau or even Cesar Cedeno? Why Wade Boggs or Roberto Clemente, only once a .300 hitter in his first five seasons, and not Harvey Kuenn, who before he was 30 was already closing fast on 2,000 hits and had one of the highest career averages since World War II?

Along with the whos and whats and whens and wheres that have definite answers, clear-cut and irrevocable answers, you will find a few whys in this book that have none. Most of them are only implied. The main purpose here is to jog the baseball mind, to rattle the cages of as many mavens out there as possible, and yet there is a possibility that a beam of light may be flung into a dark corner or two. "Hall of Fame Hot Potatoes" could do that. So for that matter could "Minor League Maestros."

In any case, you're once again assured not only of a good time as you test your knowledge of the game you love, but also of learning some new wrinkles about it. So go for those frozen ropes and taters, and lots of RB Eyes.

Take 'em all deep.

APRIL

Bottomley's Dozen

When the Dodgers hosted the Cardinals in Ebbets Field on September 16, 1924, they held second place, just a few percentage points behind the Giants, and were just coming off a 15-game winning streak. The Cards, in contrast, were buried in sixth place and merely playing out the schedule. That day the Dodgers manager started Rube Ehrhardt, a rookie righthander who had won his first five starts after being purchased in July from Lakeland in the Florida State League, and to Brooklyn's joy the St. Louis skipper countered with lefty Bill Sherdel, whom the Dodgers usually hit freely. At first base for the Cards was Jim Bottomley, then in his second major league season. Bottomley had an outside chance to hit .300 and drive in 100 runs if he put on a surge in the final fortnight of the season. By the time the day was over, he had done the following against Ehrhardt and the four pitchers who followed him for Brooklyn:

- Singled in the first inning off Ehrhardt to drive in two runs.
- Doubled in the second inning off John Hollingsworth to drive in a run.
- Hit a grand slam homer in the fourth inning off Art Decatur.
- Hit a two-run homer in the sixth inning off Decatur.
- Singled in the seventh inning off Gormer Wilson to drive in two runs.
- Singled in the ninth inning off Jim Roberts to drive in a run.

All told, Bottomley collected six hits in six at-bats, 13 total bases, and an all-time record 12 RBIs. Watching helplessly while Bottomley led the Cards to a 17–3 triumph was the Dodgers manager, who ironically had held the old record of 11 RBIs in a game, set back in 1892. For a double, can you name him? And experts would immediately take me to task if I didn't also ask who the Cardinals pilot was on that long ago September afternoon. In fact, get off to a flying start with a home run by nailing both the Hall of Fame helmsmen who witnessed Bottomley's super feat.

1. Their Niche is Secure

1. The batsman who has the highest on-base percentage of any player active since the first wave of expansion in 1961 and the only batsman since 1900 to collect 200 or more hits seven years in a row are one and the same man. Rates as an easy single.

2. He pitched for the team that scored the fewest runs of any club in its league and hence had only a 19–16 record the year he allowed just 5.26 hits per game—the lowest season average in history—as opponents hit a meager .171 against his tosses. Single for the hurler, plus an RBI for the year in question.

3. He and Ted Williams are the only two players to average more than 20 walks per 100 plate appearances during their careers. Though he and Ted were never teammates, both played their last major league games in

the same team's uniform. RBI double at max is all this one's worth.

4. He leads all shortstops in career walks with 1,302. Those who saw him well remember that he could hit that old apple too. Single.

5. The first pitcher in history to average over nine strikeouts per game (or more than one per inning) for a full season did it as a rookie. If told he repeated his feat as a soph and nearly matched it again three years later—the only other year he pitched enough to be an ERA qualifier—can you tally a single?

6. The only player active exclusively since 1961 to average .667 (two-thirds) of an RBI per game retired with a two-thirds average on the nose. Go sit in the corner if you miss this two-bagger.

7. He leads all second basemen in career RBIs with 1,599 and his name isn't Hornsby. Wager a single I can catch you napping.

8. Excluding Rod Carew, who played more at first base, who was the last to play 1,000 or more games at second base and retire with a .300+ career batting average? RBI double.

9. Ty Cobb had the highest batting average during the period from 1910–19; Rogers Hornsby led the majors in hitting during the decade of 1920s. Now name the only player in history to post the top batting average in the majors in two separate decades. Single.

10. Among all the leading hitters for each decade in major league history, who had the lowest batting average during the 10-year period he led? A can't-miss single if you know your history, but I'll credit you with two RBIs if you get his average during the decade he reigned within two points.

11. His 3,793 total bases are the most by a player who was a catcher for the vast majority of his career. No, not Berra or Bench. RBI single.

12. His 273 career RBIs lead all pitchers. Caution: we're talking about pitchers who didn't begin as or wind up as outfielders or whatever, like Joe Wood and the Babe. Rough double for some.

13. The last pitcher to win 30 or more games in consecutive seasons, he's also the last to do it three years in a row. Single for him; two RBIs if you can also nail his three-year run of greatness.

14. Among players who were stationed at third base for most of their careers, he's tops with 164 career triples. This single will be easy as pie for even fledgling historians.

15. Hop all the way to an inside-the-park homer by naming the only player among the top 20 in career triples who retired with a career slugging average below .350.

At-Bats: 15   Hits:
Potential Total Bases: 22   Total Bases:
Potential RBIs: 8   RBIs:

2. Pitching Posers

1. Cy Young made by far the most starts of any pitcher in history, but it may surprise all but our experts to discover who made the second most. Triple.

2. His best years were with Cleveland but not in the American League. He once won 14

straight games in a Cincinnati uniform but not for a National League team. And his 264 career wins are easily the most by any pitcher born in either Europe or Asia. Two bases for him; extra base for his native land.

3. There's one baseball analyst and historian who's sure to groan if he misses naming the pitcher who has the fewest career wins of any hurler in history who won 25 games in a season. Double and an RBI for the year he bagged 25.

4. He pitched his 303rd and final complete game in 1983 and figures to be the last pitcher to achieve 300+ complete games during his career. Single.

5. The last hurler to complete 40 or more games in a season was also the last to win 40 or more in a season. Single and an RBI for the year he did it.

6. Anybody in this century ever collect 45 complete games in a season? Yep, one guy did. He netted 48 but cost his team a possible pennant when he missed winning the last complete game he tossed that year. Single and an RBI for his great year.

7. After logging only seven complete games during the previous four seasons—albeit through no fault of his own—he bagged 36 and became almost undoubtedly the last hurler to amass 35 or more in a season. Understanding the clues will earn you an easy single.

8. We had no inkling at the time, but it now seems he may well have been the last pitcher to achieve as many as 30 complete games in a season. Troll for the gift clue here and grab a single, plus an RBI for the year he did it.

9. Will anyone ever complete 25 games in a season again? Seem unlikely, especially now that it's been over 10 years since it was last done, thanks to "Billy Ball." Two-bagger for the hurler.

10. And how long, for that matter, has it been since a pitcher completed 20 games in a season? Five years ago actually, and you're up for a single if you know who was the NL's top workhorse in 1986.

11. He was the only pitcher to be on an expansion team during the first year of its existence who remained with that same club for an even dozen years. Experts will fly to a double on wings that others will find too heavy even to get off the ground. Take an extra base for knowing his team.

12. Which of these southpaw slingers of the 1940s and 1950s was the only one to miss out on a cut of World Series money, largely because he never got to pitch for the Yankees? RBI single. Bobby Shantz, Bill Wight, Johnny Schmitz, Billy Hoeft, Buddy Daley, Marius Russo, Joe Ostrowski, Stubby Overmire.

13. All by himself Rube Waddell fanned nearly as many hitters in 1904 (349) as the entire pitching staff of every one of the 12 major league teams just eight years earlier. The team with the most K's in the NL that year was Pittsburgh with 362. What two Pirate hurlers finished second and third in K's in 1896? Two-run homer; single for knowing just one man.

14. Pete Dowling lost 22 games for Cleveland in 1901. Since then the Indians have had just one other 20-game loser in their long history.

Name him for a triple and take a ribby for the year he lost big just one season after he won 21.

15. Despite having had numerous cellar finishes, this team is the only one of the 16 franchises that have been in existence since 1901 that's had just one pitcher lose 20 games in a season. He dropped 21 for a basement dweller the year after he won 20 for a seventh-place club that finished two games ahead of the last team managed by Frankie Frisch. Single for the team; two RBIs for him.

At-Bats: 15   Hits:
Potential Total Bases: 28   Total Bases:
Potential RBIs: 10   RBIs:

3. Dynamite Duos

1. Their combined total of 347 RBIs in 1931 are a teammate duo record. Need 'em both for a single.

2. They set an NL teammate duo record in 1930 when they combined for 324 RBIs. RBI single, but give yourself a sac hit if you know just one of them.

3. Here's a belated clue. One of the above-cited men had a share of the old NL record of 308 RBIs, set one year earlier with another heavy hitter of the time. This duo's worth two.

4. The last pair of teammates to collect 100+ homers in a season between them, they set an all-time duo record when they sailed 115 balls into the seats in fair territory. Gotta have both for a single.

5. Their 326 combined RBIs are the most by any pair of teammates since 1931. This may prove a tough triple even after I throw in that neither man led the league in ribbies that year.

6. Their 91 homers in 1965 set a new NL teammates' mark and shattered the old duo record of 87, set by two members of a team representing the same franchise 18 years earlier. Single for the new record setters; two extra bases for the old pair.

7. The first teammate duo to top 100 homers in a season, their mark of 107 stood unchallenged for 34 years. Need both the pair and the year they topped 100 to score a single.

8. The first pair of teammates to finish 1–2 in RBIs in the NL after the mound was moved to its present distance from the plate, they played together just one more season before each jumped to an AL team that offered more money. Two bases for the pair; RBI for the year they led.

9. Who were the first pair of teammates to finish 1–2 in RBIs in the AL? Your clues are that they totaled just 160 RBIs between them for a flag winner that topped the junior circuit with 623 runs scored, the fewest ever to lead the AL (1918 excepted). Triple for both; sac hit if you know just their team.

10. They were the last pair of teammates prior to Kevin Mitchell and Will Clark to finish 1–2 in RBIs for a flag winner. RBI single.

11. Only once, in 1932, have players representing teams in the same city finished 1–2 in RBIs in both leagues. Knowing that neither team won a pennant that year should be clue

enough. Sac hit for the city; homer if you know all four sluggers concerned.

12. Just once in major league history have three players from the same team finished 1–2–3 in RBIs for a pennant winner. The trio and team rate an RBI double.

13. What was the only team that *failed* to win the pennant despite having the three top RBI men in its league that year? Single for the team; homer if you also know its slugging trio, who combined for 323 RBIs but only 10 home runs.

14. The only team except the 1949 Red Sox to have the two top men in RBIs, plus the top two men in homers, and yet fail to win the flag also had three 20-game winners! Single for the team; two extra bases for its two slugging duos; a two-run homer if you also know the 20-game winners.

15. Neither member of the only pair of team- mates ever to finish 1–2 in RBIs in their league *four years in a row* ever played on a World Championship team. Now that Ruth and Gehrig are out of the way, get down to business and end with a neat double here.

At-Bats: 15   Hits:
Potential Total Bases: 34   Total Bases:
Potential RBIs: 7   RBIs:

4. All in the Family

1. The Waners both made the Hall of Fame but never finished 1–2 in a league batting title race. These two brothers did. Their name

brings a bingle; the year they dominated rates an RBI.

2. In the spring of 1986 it seemed as if the McRaes, Hal and Brian, would become the first father-son duo to be active in the majors in the same season, but this pair became the first instead. Single.

3. Who were the only brothers both to be named to the *Sporting News* All-Star team in a year that they were teammates? Your clue is that one sib won 22 games in 1942 while wearing a different uniform number each time he pitched, corresponding to which number victory he was seeking that day. Two-bagger.

4. What brothers opposed each other while playing on the two teams that vied for the 1933 AL pennant after playing for many years as teammates on yet a third AL team? Single, plus an RBI for knowing their clubs in 1933.

5. The Niekros and the Perrys lead all brother acts in every significant career pitching department except complete games. For a triple, what trio of brothers heads that list?

6. Even after his brother's career total is deducted, he still has more career home runs all by himself than any sibling pair, trio, or even quintet. Single.

7. They and the Ferrells are the only brother duos both halves of which had lengthy major league careers which saw the pitching half top the everyday-player half in both career home runs and career batting average. Solo homer.

8. In 1988 the Ripkens became the first sibling

keystone combo to play regularly for the same team for a full season. Who were the first brothers to play together at shortstop and second base in a 20th century ML game? Your clue is the year they did it, the second base half became the first player to bat under artificial lights in a major league game. Grand slam homer if you know both brothers, their team, and the year in question. Single for the second sacker.

9. The only trio of brothers to make their big league debuts in three different decades, the eldest had the greatest day of anybody who played just one major league game, a second was once an AL batting title runner-up, and the third made his first major league appearance 24 years after the eldest brother made his. Single for the family name; two extra bases if you also know all three of their first names.

10. It was brother against brother in the 1985 American League Championship Series. The elder sib, who got into the fray only as a pinch hitter, won out and then delivered the key blow in that year's World Series, the two-run pinch single that won Game 6. RBI single.

11. His grandfather knocked home 102 runs as a rookie third sacker with the 1936 Pirates; he topped the 1986 Yankees with 18 wins. Single for the grandson; two-run homer for both.

12. They lead all father–son combos in career homers. Single.

13. Not only were they the first brothers to play in the same outfield, they each hit .275 the lone year they were teammate regulars. The

elder's in the Hall of Fame and the younger nearly won the NL bat title as a rookie. RBI double.

14. All-around sports fans will bag a two-run homer here; others of you may be stopped dead in your tracks when asked who were the first pair of brothers to play in a World Series game and an NFL Championship game? They did it three years apart, the baseball sib for a club that met a team in the Series that bore the same nickname but (at that time anyway) did not represent the same city as his brother's NFL eleven.

At-Bats: 14   Hits:
Potential Total Bases: 32 Total Bases:
Potential RBIs: 13   RBIs:

5. Batting Title Bafflers

1. Dale Alexander and Richie Ashburn were the first players whose last names began with *A* to lead the AL and the NL respectively in batting since 1920. What even more significant post-deadball-first distinction do they share? Wicked era RBI double.

2. When Kirby Puckett and Carney Lansford finished 1–2 in the AL batting race in 1989, it marked the first time (except for the abbreviated 1981 season) since when that two righty hitters had topped the AL? Huge clue: they were teammates. Need both for a deuce.

3. He was the last righty hitter to win back-to-back batting titles. Worth two.

4. Who was the last righty hitter to win a Triple Crown? Single.

5. He won his only bat title in part because he spent most of the tag end of the season on the disabled list, thus freezing his average at .344, but returned to lead his club in the World Series that year with a .333 average. Take two for him; an RBI for the year.

6. His lone bat crown came at the expense of Joe Vosmik, who began the final day of the season on the bench to protect a slender batting lead and then was rushed in vain into action when word came that our man had gotten a rash of hits in his season-closing game. RBI triple.

7. He came the closest of any DH to winning a bat title when he cracked .332 in 1976, only to lose the crown to a teammate by a single point. Double.

8. He was the last player in an A's uniform—Philadelphia, Kansas City, Oakland, whatever—to win a batting title. Double for him; RBI for the year an A last won.

9. The only two St. Louis Browns players to win batting crowns both had the same first name, and you need both to score a two-bagger.

10. He's the only member of his team to win a batting title and the lone AL shortstop to cop two crowns. Single.

11. What Hall of Famer's 140 total bases and 102 hits are the fewest by a batting title winner in any year except the strike-shortened 1981 season? Two bases for him; extra base for the year it happened.

12. The last NL player to win a batting title without hitting a single homer, he had just 21 more total bases (158) than hits (137), the smallest differential ever by a bat crown winner. Ironically, he'd led the NL in total bases only two years earlier. Two-run double.

13. His 450 total bases are the most in a season by a batting crown winner. Single for him; RBI for the year he did it.

14. He's the only player to win a batting title and hit 50 or more homers in the same season he triumphed. One for him; extra base for the year he did it.

At-Bats: 14   Hits:
Potential Total Bases: 26   Total Bases:
Potential RBIs: 7   RBIs:

6. The Magic Circle

All of the pitchers you'll meet here were either record-setting 20-game winners or losers—and some were both!

1. The only pitcher since the end of the dead-ball era to win 20 or more games at least nine times, he did it in no fewer than 13 seasons. One base.

2. Oldies buffs will polish off a solo homer by naming the only pitcher in history to win 20 games seven or more times in a season and yet finish with less than 200 career wins.

The only other clue you should need is he copped 47 victories in 1884.

3. He's the only hurler in big league history to win 20 games more than ten times but never play on a pennant winner. Double.

4. There were no 20-game winners in 1981 owing to the long strike and just one in 1982. Told that he won 23 that year and led the majors in shutouts, you should trot to a single.

5. The only AL hurler to win 20 in either 1959 or 1960, he racked up 22 victories for the last Windy City flag winner. Single.

6. The NL's lone 20-game winner in 1952, he set a post-World War II NL record when he bagged 28 victories. Single.

7. The last year that a lefty won 30 games was also the first year that no NL pitcher won as many as 20. Single for the year; each of the three hurlers who tied for the NL lead that year with 19 wins rates an RBI.

8. He lost 20 games three times for a record three different teams. Double, plus an RBI for each team that suffered with him.

9. Which one of the following Hall of Famers never lost 20 games in a season? Single. Walter Johnson, Cy Young, Red Ruffing, Ted Lyons, Eppa Rixey, Robin Roberts, Earl Wynn, Mickey Welch, Hoss Radbourn, John Clarkson.

10. He was the last pitcher to lose 20 or more games two years in a row. Two bases, plus an RBI for the years in question.

11. In 1954 the Indians had five pitchers who won 20 or more games in a season during their careers at least twice each and produced among them a grand total of twenty-

four 20-win seasons, a post-deadball record for a pitching staff. Two-bagger for all five hurlers; sac hit for less.

12. The only AL hurler to win more than 20 games in a season between 1955 and 1957, he bagged 21 in 1956 for a Hall of Fame manager who was serving as a pilot for his 29th and last season. Double, plus an RBI for his manager.

13. The only pitcher in the past 20 years to win 20 games two years in a row for a second-division team did it in 1975–76. RBI single.

14. What pitcher in 1966 became the first since Walter Johnson in 1917 to win 20 games in back-to-back years for a second-division team? Your clue is that he played on three flag winners during that decade but only once won 20 on a flag-winning team. Single.

At-Bats: 14   Hits:
Potential Total Bases: 22   Total Bases:
Potential RBIs: 6   RBIs:

7. Home Run Leaders

1. Three players in the 20th century have won NL home run crowns with two different teams. You need the entire trio for an RBI double.

2. Who is the only slugger to win a league home run crown with three different teams? Single for him, plus an RBI if you nail all three teams.

3. Who is the only slugger to lead both major

leagues in homers during this century? RBI single.

4. There have been numerous times that two players have tied for a league home run crown, but only on one occasion have four players shared one. The circumstances that year were special, and so will you be if you can identify the year for a single and collect an RBI for knowing at least three of the four players concerned.

5. He was the last to lead the NL in four-baggers while hitting fewer than 30 home runs. Might have been tough if I hadn't, in a weak moment, decided to throw in that he was also the last rookie to top the NL in homers. Single.

6. Four Yankees between 1920 and 1940 won home run crowns. Three are a snap; the fourth may take some musing. Need all for a double.

7. Harmon Killebrew and he are the only sluggers to lead the AL in homers on two separate occasions despite batting under .250. RBI single.

8. He was the last home run leader who also finished among the top five in his league that year in batting. Jim Rice would be a great guess, but our man did it after Rice. Single.

9. Prior to Babe Ruth's arrival, he was the only player to be a league leader in homers for four or more consecutive seasons. Your clues are his first four-bagger came in a Giants uniform, he hit just 74 all told, and his homer crowns all came after 1900. Homer, plus an extra RBI for his period of domination.

10. Who is the only catcher in this century to

be a league leader in homers? Easy bingle, but can you pick up an RBI for knowing the years he did it?

11. The only lefty swinger to win a home run crown for the Cubs since the end of the deadball era, he held the club southpaw homer record until Billy Williams broke it. RBI double.

12. The only Cincinnati player to win back-to-back home run crowns never won another. Single, plus an RBI for the years he won.

13. Brooklyn had many great sluggers, but only one man won two home run crowns while wearing a Brooklyn uniform. Just knowing he's worth a two-run homer ought to tell you we're not talking here about anybody like Snider or Hodges.

14. Ty Cobb and Sam Crawford led the AL in homers in consecutive seasons (1908–09). Who was the next Tigers player to win a home run crown? RBI single.

15. Four players were league home run leaders both prior to and subsequent to World War II. All are in the Hall of Fame, but you're in for a zero instead of a two-run double if you don't know the entire quartet.

At-Bats: 15   Hits:
Potential Total Bases: 25   Total Bases:
Potential RBIs: 15   RBIs:

MAY

The Short-Lived Record

The first complete game a certain Houston right-hander hurled in his major league career was a 2–0 two-hit shutout in which he fanned 10 men. But all but two of his 10 K's came in the first three innings, as our man began the game by fanning the first eight batters he faced, a modern record and only one shy of the all-time record for the most consecutive strikeouts by a pitcher at the start of a game, before pinch hitter Larry See, batting for rival pitcher Dennis Powell, broke his skein by popping out. It's worth a double if you know the Astros pitcher we're talking about here. Take an extra base by nailing the year the event under discussion occurred and the team that See and Powell played for. Now, what about that all-time record-holder whose mark of nine K's was seriously threatened that day for the first time in a century? Well, I'll clue you that he won over 300 games in the majors and still award two RBIs for his name. Oh, and by the way, claim a grand slam homer if you also remember the White Sox flinger who on May 28 of the year in question had set a new modern record of seven consecutive strikeouts at the start of a game, only to see his mark shattered less than five months later by the Houston fireballer!

8. No-Hitter Nuggets

1. The first hurler in the 20th century to throw three no-hitters, he still holds the AL record for the most complete-game one-hitters with 12. Single.

2. He was the second pitcher in history to toss two no-hitters in a season and the first to do it in the junior circuit. Single.

3. The only AL pitcher ever to follow a no-hitter with a one-hitter, he did it on September 11, 1923, for the Red Sox, and many witnesses swore that the lone hit he surrendered that day, an infield single by the Yankees' lead batter, should have been an error charged to his third baseman. Double.

4. He began the 1934 season by throwing a one-hitter on Opening Day for the Cubs and then gave up just a single hit again in his next start. Really humming them in April—he opened with five straight wins—he slowed down a trifle but still posted 22 victories. And, yes, in 1941 he finally got his first no-hitter. Two-run single.

5. The holder of the record for the fewest hits allowed (3) in three consecutive games gave up all three safe blows on June 15, 1938. Plenty there to single on.

6. He's the only pitcher to throw a no-hitter in four consecutive seasons. One base.

7. The year after he became the first pitcher to heave three one-hitters in a season from a mound at its present distance from the plate, he hurled the only perfect game ever

achieved in the heat of a late-season pennant race. RBI single.

8. In 1892, appearing in his first major league game, he pitched a no-hitter on the latest date ever, October 15, as he beat Pittsburgh, 7–1. It was his lone big league win and the last no-hitter thrown from a pitcher's box only 50 feet away from home plate. Two-bagger.

9. Your eye for intriguing records has to be sharper than an eagle's if you know not only the above man but also the first pitcher to throw a no-hitter from a mound 60'6" from the plate. He did it for Baltimore on August 16, 1893. Triple.

10. The first chucker to throw a no-hitter in an AL contest at the same time also became the first ever to lose a no-hit game that went at least nine innings when the White Sox came on in the 10th frame to top his Cleveland crew, 4–2, on May 9, 1901. RBI double.

11. The first pitcher to chalk up a no-hitter for an expansion team was none other than Mamie's main man at the time. RBI single.

12. This Hall of Famer's first no-hitter, a 1–0 win in 1880, came while pitching from a box just 45 feet from the plate. His second, four years later from a box that was now 50 feet away, was an 18–0 whitewash, the most lop-sided no-hit win in history. Toiling for the same team on both occasions, he's the only man to throw a no-hitter for a major league outfit representing the city that holds the current minor league season attendance record. Single, plus an RBI for the city.

13. The only year during the deadball era

(1901–19) that no ML pitcher threw a no-hitter was the season that Jake Daubert copped his first of two straight batting titles. Two bases for the year.

14. Which one of the following Hall of Famers never threw a no-hitter? Single. Christy Mathewson, Bob Lemon, Pete Alexander, Walter Johnson, Carl Hubbell, Ted Lyons, Bob Gibson, Hoyt Wilhelm, Amos Rusie.

15. When the Phillies' Jim Bunning fashioned a perfect game in 1964, how many years had it been since an NL hurler had last achieved a perfect-game victory? Triple.

At-Bats: 15   Hits:
Potential Total Bases: 23   Total Bases:
Potential RBIs: 5   RBIs:

9. Silver Sluggers

1. He holds the record for the most homers by a player who hit .400 or better that same season. Single, plus an RBI for his super silver year.

2. In 1927, when Ruth all by himself outhomered every opposing AL team and Gehrig outhomered four of the other seven AL clubs, what two sluggers on a Manhattan-based New York team accounted for a combined 46 homers to make them the year's second-best slugging duo? Need both for a double.

3. Who broke Babe Ruth's Red Sox season

home run record of 29, set in 1919? Double, plus an RBI for the year the mark fell.

4. Of the 20th-century players who have hit four home runs in a single game, he had the fewest homers (19) during the season in which he did it. Double.

5. His 159 hits are the fewest by any player who hit 50 or more home runs in that same season. RBI single.

6. What player once had a season in which he had only 91 official at-bats but nevertheless hit 13 homers and collected 34 walks? Some incredible pinch hitter, this guy? No, just an incredible hitter. Single.

7. He's the only player in major league history whose first three hits were all home runs. He did it in 1949 after the Phils called him up from the minors in September, and he never hit another four-bagger in top company. Three-run homer.

8. He once had a season in which he averaged 10.5 home runs per 100 at-bats, the fourth highest average in history—yet failed to lead his team, let alone his league in homers that year. Need him and the year for an RBI single.

9. John Milner in an otherwise undistinguished career hit 131 home runs, but 10 were grand slams. Only one other player who hit fewer than 200 career home runs connected for 10 or more grand slams. Our man made 12 of his 179 four-baggers worth four runs and had a much more lustrous career than Milner. But even after telling you he starred on a team that won three con-

secutive World Championships, I'll wager a double you don't know him.

10. At the conclusion of the 1929 season, he held the 20th-century season home run record for three different clubs and just a year earlier had held still a fourth club's record. Name him for a single; an RBI for each of the three teams you know whose record he held going into the 1930 season; two extra bases for knowing what player in 1929 broke the fourth record he'd previously held, and the player who took another team mark from him in 1930.

11. What two currently active players led the AL and the NL respectively in total bases in consecutive seasons but have never been home run leaders? Your clue is they each did it in the same two seasons. Double, plus an RBI for the years.

12. He's the only member of the 500 home run club who was a league leader in homers on just one occasion during his career. RBI single.

13. He holds the record for the most homers in a season by a player wearing a Milwaukee uniform and also is the Braves' all-time season franchise record holder. Single for him; RBI for the year he garnered both records.

14. He will always hold the Seattle Pilots' season and career records for both the most home runs and the most RBIs. RBI triple.

At-Bats: 14	Hits:
Potential Total Bases: 26	Total Bases:
Potential RBIs: 13	RBIs:

10. Terrific Tandems

1. This mound pair won an AL-record 64 games between them, but their team lost the flag that year on the last day of the season when one member of the tandem was tagged with his 12th loss rather than gaining his 42nd win. Need both for a triple.

2. The last team to have two pitchers who won over 55 games combined was also the only AL team since 1912 to have two hurlers who won 55+ games between them and failed to win the pennant. Two for the team, extra base for the pitchers.

3. The last NL team to fail to win a pennant despite having two pitchers who won 50 games between them finished second to a team that was winning its third straight flag that year without having a 20-game winner. Parlay that clue into a triple for the team, plus an RBI apiece for its two mound aces.

4. They were the first tandem in history to finish 1–2 in a major league in wins and yet fail to pitch for a pennant winner. Moreover, the best their combined 64 victories could earn was fourth place. Now wait, this gets better. The win leader that year with 34 had had 34 losses the year before to lead the American Association (then a major league). And the other pitcher had headed the Association two years earlier with 45 wins while playing under the same manager who skippered the fourth-place club. Tough even with all those clues, so you get a two-run homer if you can scope out the two pitchers,

the league they led in wins, and their manager. Two-bagger for anything less.

5. Their combined 49 wins are the most by any
NL tandem since expansion. They did it for
a flag winner, and the top man won 26 games
and fanned 106 more batters than Bob Veale,
the runner-up to him in K's that year. Two
bases.

6. They set a 20th-century record when they
combined for 68 wins one season. Their
team won the flag but didn't appear in a
World Series that fall. Double.

7. In 1920 the White Sox had four 20-game
winners who won a combined 87 games;
Cleveland in contrast got only 83 wins from
its top four hurlers but took the flag when
two of the quartet kicked in 55 wins
between them. Two for the Tribe's big two
that year.

8. This team began each of three consecutive
decades with the top pitching tandem in its
league. But on one occasion, that amounted
to just 33 wins and in only one of the three
instances did the team win a flag. One base
for the team and the three decade-beginning
seasons; two RBIs for the tandem that led
with 33 wins.

9. This team's four main starters won 82 games
all told in 1923, including a major league
high of 48 by its top tandem, but the club
finished second largely because its second-
line hurlers netted just nine wins. Single for
the team; two extra bases for its terrific
tandem.

10. They amassed 77 wins between them, the
all-time tandem record. Moreover, one of

them won 24 games that year in another major league, giving them an incredible grand total of 101 combined victories. Knowing that the second man's defection to a rival circuit was responsible for the first man's being reinstated as his club's ace should get you both the team and the hurlers for an RBI double.

11. Their 36 wins for the last-place_____ in_____ tied the 20th-century record, set 73 years earlier by Noodles Hahn and Bill Phillips of the Reds, for the most victories by a tandem pitching for a last-place team. The year in question one member of the tandem also set a new AL record for the most wins by a pitcher on a cellar dweller. Now get the team, the year, and the tandem for an RBI double.

12. This pair of chuckers one year combined for 52 losses and just eight wins, four apiece. But their eight wins made them their team's top tandem—and the lamest top tandem in history. Single for the team; homer if you know both pitchers.

13. In 1946 this team had the major's top tandem with a combined 45 wins and copped a runaway pennant. Three years later the club again had the best tandem going as a different pair won 48 games between them. This time, however, the team could do no better than second place. Single for the team; homer if in addition you score all four members of its two top tandems.

14. The 1947–64 Yankees, winners of 15 pennants in 18 years, had the top pitching tandem in the majors just once during their

long span of domination. And that, ironically, was the season they did the poorest of any Bomber team to that date in World Series action. Single for the year; extra base for the top tandem.

At-Bats: 14   Hits:
Potential Total Bases: 37   Total Bases:
Potential RBIs: 10   RBIs:

11. Managerial Musings

1. Among the 16 franchises in existence since 1901, which one has had the fewest managers? Single, plus two extra bases if you zap the lone skipper who served just one year at this team's helm.
2. Connie Mack naturally holds the record for the most uninterrupted years of service as a manager of the same AL team. Who ranks second to Mack among AL managers? Single, plus an extra base for knowing the years he served.
3. What was the only NL team to have the same manager on Opening Day in 1906 who was at its helm on Opening Day in 1901? Single, plus an RBI for its skipper.
4. Three managers in this century have at various times been at the reins of six different clubs. One won pennants with three of his six crews; one won a flag with one and a division title with a second; and the third won zip. Now name all three for a homer.

5. He alone among all managers in history led three different clubs to pennants in the same league. Single for him; extra base for each club he piloted to a flag.

6. Excepting the years when the Cubs played musical chairs with their manager's post, what's the only club in the 20th century to have as many as four managers in the same season? Single for the team; two-run homer if you can also punch out the names of all four skippers.

7. He was the first ex-big league pitcher to win a flag in this century at the helm of an NL team. Tough solo homer.

8. Who was the first man to play a full season under a mentor named John McGraw and later manage a pennant winner himself? Double.

9. Next, who was the first man to play a full season under Connie Mack's tutelage and later manage a pennant winner himself? Take two more bases.

10. Only one pitcher in this century has won a flag as a player-manager. Name him for a double, plus an RBI for his club.

11. Which of the following pennant-winning player-managers is the only one who later won a flag for a club he skippered while no longer an active player? Single. Lou Boudreau, Fielder Jones, Frank Chance, Mickey Cochrane, Rogers Hornsby, Gabby Hartnett, Tris Speaker, Bucky Harris, Fred Clarke, Frankie Frisch.

12. Who was the last outfielder to win a flag while serving as a player-manager? RBI single, plus an extra base for the year he did it.

13. Hugh Jennings was the first former shortstop to win a flag in this century as a manager, but he was never really a regular
shortstop after 1900. Who was the first post-
1900 shortstop to subsequently win a pennant as a manager in either the NL or the
AL? RBI double.

14. Jimmy Collins and John McGraw were the
first two third basemen to manage pennant
winners in this century. Who was the next
ex-big league third sacker to pilot a flag winner? Two bases, plus an extra base for the
year he first did it.

At-Bats: 14   Hits:
Potential Total Bases: 34   Total Bases:
Potential RBIs: 8   RBIs:

12. Their Niche is Secure

1. If told that he has the same last name as a
Hall of Fame hurler and that he's the only
pitcher since 1942 to have a season in which
he issued less than one walk per game in
over 200 innings, can you snag him for a single? Plus an RBI if you know his super control year.

2. His 1,732 career RBIs lead all shortstops by
a wide margin. Single.

3. He leads all catchers with 1,430 career RBIs.
Guaranteed, some will stumble here. Single.

4. Among retired players who were active

exclusively after 1930, his career batting average of .344 is the highest. Single.

5. His .320 career batting average tops all catchers. Single.

6. Among catchers who worked 1,000 or more games behind the plate and were active exclusively after World War II, his career batting average of .296 is the best. No trickery here; this man's a bona fide catcher, not somebody like Joe Torre, who also played a lot at other positions. Double.

7. In the same year that he gave up the most walks of any lefty in the 20th century, he allowed the *fewest* hits per game of *any* hurler in *any* season between the end of the deadball era and expansion. The walk clue makes this rate as only a single.

8. Until Sandy Koufax did it in 1963–65, he was the lone pitcher since 1893 to fan 900 batters (an average of 300 or more per season) over a three-year span. Single for him; two ribbies for the years he did it.

9. He was the first black hurler to win 20 or more games in a season for an AL team. RBI single; extra ribby for the year he did it.

10. He tops all catchers in career walks with 984, although he also played other positions at times. What's more, he holds the AL record for the lowest season batting average (.211) by a player who collected over 100 walks. RBI single.

11. He was the only player active exclusively before 1900 to accumulate over 1,000 career walks and was therefore the first in history to do it. He's much better known, though, for another career offensive department

record he once held. Need both him and the other record for a double.

12. Who are the only three shortstops among the top 50 in career batting average? Gotta have 'em all to score a single here.

13. In 1913, while enjoying perhaps the greatest year any pitcher's ever had, he posted an all-time record when he held opponents to a mere .217 on-base percentage. Single.

14. The last pitcher to lose 25 games or more in a season did it while pitching for the last team to start the year with Babe Ruth on its active roster. Two-bagger, but just a sac hit if you know only the team.

15. Only once in major league history has a pitcher won 30 games and hit .300 or better that same season with over 100 hits. He did it for a flag winner—and in the same year that another pitcher in his league won the circuit's batting crown. For a homer, name both men and the year that hurlers stole the whole show; single if you know just one of the pitchers.

At-Bats: 15   Hits:
Potential Total Bases: 21   Total Bases:
Potential RBIs: 7   RBIs:

13. Great Glovemen

1. He won the first Gold Glove ever given to a pitcher and went on to bag eight all told, four in each league, while playing for four different teams. That's a record right there,

and he has another; he's the only pitcher to win an MVP Award while playing for a team that finished lower than second in either its league or division. Take two.

2. The first first sacker to sweep as many as seven Gold Gloves in a row never saw World Series action. RBI single.

3. Dig in your spikes and slam a stand-up double by naming the only two brothers to win Gold Gloves at the same position. Single.

4. He won three Gold Gloves in a row, including the first ever awarded to a player at his position, before giving way to a player who would go on to cop a record 16 consecutive Gold Gloves. He rates three; his GG heir will get you a sac hit should you whiff on him.

5. He won three Gold Gloves as an outfielder but played shortstop in his only taste of World Series play. Two-run double.

6. No Cleveland shortstop, second baseman, or third baseman has ever won a Gold Glove. Knowing that, can you nail the last Tribesman to win one at *any* position? Three-bagger.

7. He's the only lefty catcher in history to win a Gold Glove. Hope you're shrewd enough to have already figured out on your own that he got it for playing another position. Two for him, plus an RBI for the year he triumphed.

8. His four Gold Gloves make him the only outfielder in NL history who was neither black nor Latino to win more than one. Just a single.

9. In 1960 all four Gold Glove performers at

the two keystone positions save one played
for teams based in the same city. Who was
the odd man out who prevented a keystone
sweep by that city? Sac hit for the city; double for knowing its three keystone aces that
year as well as the lone fly in the ointment.

10. Frankly put, he was the only righty pitcher
prior to 1965 to win a Gold Glove—and the
only AL righty prior to 1976. RBI double.

11. Of these four standout white center fielders
of the 1950s and early 1960s, which one won
twice as many Gold Gloves as the other
three combined? Single. Richie Ashburn,
Jimmy Piersall, Mickey Mantle, Duke
Snider.

12. In 1978 he ended the consecutive ten-year
NL reign of a Hall of Famer when he garnered his first Gold Glove; in 1982 he ended
the consecutive six-year AL reign of another
player by taking his first Gold Glove in the
junior loop. Single, plus an RBI if you know
both of the crack glovemen whose skeins he
interrupted.

At-Bats: 12   Hits:
Potential Total Bases: 20   Total Bases:
Potential RBIs: 5   RBIs:

14. Team Teasers

1. The last team to fashion a winning streak as
long as 16 games, in so doing it set a new
season record for wins by an AL West team

and copped an easy division flag—but not a pennant. Single for the team, plus an RBI for the year.

2. Two years after this team won the second pennant in its history, it plummeted to the basement as it lost a pre-1988 AL record 20 straight games, 19 of them at home. Two bases for the team; RBI for the year.

3. What team was disbanded after it had losing steaks of 24, 16, and 14 games in the course of its final season in the majors? Two-bagger.

4. Six of the 16 original franchises that existed unchanged from 1903–52 have since moved to new cities. Which of the six had the best overall 20th-century record in its old domicile? Single.

5. When _____ whacked 33 four-baggers in 1971, he became the first member of which of the original 16 franchises to be a league home run leader? Single for the team; two extra bases for its breakthrough slugger.

6. Ken Williams was the only player from what team to lead the AL in homers in a year when the country was not at war? Single for the team; RBI for the year he interrupted the Babe's dominance.

7. This team had the AL's top home run hitter five times in the 1950s but hasn't had a four-bagger leader since 1959. Single.

8. In 1950, when there were an all-time record-low 278 steals in the AL, the team that was last in thefts turned around its image so swiftly that it led the loop the following year, while one of the teams that tied for first in 1950 with 42 thefts would nab an all-time record low of 13 just seven years later.

Name both clubs for a double; sac hit for just one.

9. What was the last team to win 100 or more games three years in a row? Single, plus an RBI for the years it romped.

10. Now, how about the only NL team to win 100 or more games three years running? The streak brought it three flags and two World Championships. Single, plus an RBI for its glory years.

11. And next, what team won a record 322 games over a three-year period but failed to win 100 games three years in a row? The club did win three successive flags, however, only to miss out on a fourth despite registering 104 victories to give it an additional record of 426 wins in a four-year stretch. Single for the team; RBI for its four-year period of dominance.

12. What club suffered the most losses in a season of any team in this century despite playing two less games than the schedule called for? Single.

13. This team finished in the first division a record 39 straight years before experiencing a keen disappointment when it tried for 40 in a row. The clues are there to give you both the club and the year it finally stumbled for a single.

14. What pennant-winning team holds the all-time record for being in first place the fewest days during the regular season? Telling you the club needed a playoff to triumph knocks this down to a single.

15. This team set an unwanted AL record when it won only nine games one year by one run

and was a dismal 9–18 in one-run games.
But surprise—despite its ineffectiveness in
one-run games, the team won the World
Series that year. After losing a one-run 1–0
game in the opener! Triple.

At-Bats: 15   Hits:
Potential Total Bases: 22   Total Bases:
Potential RBIs: 6   RBIs:

JUNE

The Enigmatic Walk Leaders

They first played in the majors as teammates the last season that the two largest cities east of the Mississippi met in a World Series. Following World War II, they were reunited for the first time in eight years and shared the first base job on the team with which both of them had begun their major league careers. The next year one of the pair set an AL record for the most walks in a season by a first baseman. His ex-teammate meanwhile led the NL in walks. Neither man ever played another game in the major leagues after that season. The clues are there for the savvy to figure out who both men are and reel in a triple. Bloop single if you know only the Hall of Fame half of the pair.

15. Pitching Posers

1. The only pitcher since 1900 to average 44 + starts over a five-year span made 224 starts during that period and, no, he's not somebody your great-grandfather saw play. Matter of fact, many of you did. RBI single.
2. Which of the following Hall of Fame hurlers was the only one to bag 200 or more career victories? Single. Ed Walsh, Chief Bender, Addie Joss, Sandy Koufax, Rube Waddell,

Hoyt Wilhelm, Jack Chesbro, Dazzy Vance, Dizzy Dean.

3. Yaz put in a club-record 23 years with the Red Sox. Bob Stanley holds the Sox record for the most seasons by a pitcher (13). Prior to Stanley's arrival, who was the only hurler ever to be with the Red Sox more than ten seasons? Your clues are that he had an 84–75 career record overall but was a glittering 34–15 as a reliever. Double.

4. The Milwaukee Braves were extant only 13 years, but he won 235 games for them—far more than the leaders of most teams that have been around the entire century. What's more, he's tied with Dick Rudolph for the most wins (122) by a Boston Braves hurler. Single.

5. Like the Milwaukee Braves, the Kansas City A's were with us just 13 seasons. Unlike the Braves, their career wins leader had a measly 39. Name him for a homer.

6. The career wins leader for the expansion Washington Senators had just 49 victories. If told that he also holds the club record for the most wins in a season, 16 in 1970, can you snare him for an RBI double?

7. He leads all Minnesota Twins hurlers in career wins with 189. Single.

8. Joe Niekro leads all Astros hurlers with 144 career wins. What pitcher leads the 'stros in years of service, games, innings, starts, and complete games? Double.

9. The Royals' leader in career wins with 166 may surprise all but KC followers, who'll remember his long and quietly successful tenure with the team. RBI single.

10. The only hurler to win over 200 games in a Cubs uniform, he picked up 201 victories as a Bruin. RBI double.

11. The lone hurler to win 200 games or more for the Pirates was a southpaw who never pitched on a flag winner. Two-run single.

12. The BoSox leader in career wins collected 193 despite the fact that he pitched just eight years for the Hose. Single.

13. His 126 wins in a Browns uniform are the fewest by a career wins leader among all AL teams except expansion franchises. RBI single.

14. No Browns pitcher ever led the AL in ERA, and only two had the second-best ERA. One was Ned Garver in 1950; the other did it back in 1906 and rates a three-run homer.

15. It should come as no great surprise that his 149 K's in 1922 made him the only St. Louis Browns hurler ever to lead the AL in strikeouts. Two-bagger.

At-Bats: 15   Hits:
Potential Total Bases: 23   Total Bases:
Potential RBIs: 11   RBIs:

16. Their Niche Is Secure

1. Wade Boggs was the first player since Ted Williams to carry a .350+ career batting average after his first eight seasons. Who was the last player prior to Williams to do it?

Your only clue is he had a .363 average after his eighth campaign. RBI single.

2. The only catcher to post a .500 or better career slugging average finished at exactly .500. Single.

3. Who is second among catchers with a .489 career slugging average? Double.

4. Excluding Ernie Banks, who played half his career at first base, who has the record for the highest career slugging average (.460) by a shortstop? Two-bagger.

5. The only player since 1931 to rap as many as 23 triples in a season also ranks among the ten hardest batters in history to fan, even though he ended his career with a famous strikeout. Double, plus an RBI if you know the circumstances surrounding his last at-bat.

6. In 1930, when he collected a record 190 RBIs, Hack Wilson averaged a post-1900 record 1.23 RBIs per game. Who else that same season became the only other player since 1900 to average as many as 1.20 RBIs per game? Big hint: he led neither league that year in RBIs. Single.

7. The last man to play over 130 games in a season in which he averaged better than one RBI per game was a rookie who finished his career with an average of .547 RBIs per game, about half of the 1.06 he averaged as a frosh. Solo homer.

8. The only shortstop since 1893 to top the .400 barrier for a full season, he stroked .401 after banging .386 the previous year. Yep, he's in the HOF, but he might not be if his

playing accomplishments were all he'd had going for him. RBI single.

9. His .491 on-base percentage the year he played behind Cy Blanton, the NL's ERA leader, is the highest in history by a short-stop. Single, plus an RBI for the season he did it.

10. Ty Cobb leads the AL with a .366 career batting average; Hornsby has the NL's high-est career batting average counting only his years in the senior loop; Benny Kauff holds the Federal League record; Pete Browning the Players League mark. Who is the only player to lead a major league with a career batting average of .400+ in that circuit? Two-bagger.

11. Will White, in 1879, was the last pitcher to win 100% of his team's victories. Take two for knowing the last pitcher to win 50% of his team's triumphs, plus an RBI for the year it occurred.

12. He led all AL outfielders with 16 assists in 1961, and seven years later, when pressed into service on the mound, he became the last non-pitcher to win a major league game. RBI single.

13. Numerologists will make much of it when they discover the year that this hurler set an all-time record when he held opposing hitters to a .168 batting average, and Cleve-land fans of that vintage will snag an easy RBI single.

14. George Brett's super .390 season in 1980 is the top batting average by a third baseman since 1900. Who previously held the AL

record for the highest season batting average
by a third sacker? Two-run triple.

15. In 1918 he hit .300 in over 400 at-bats but
scored just 37 runs, hit no homers, and had
only 29 RBIs, giving him the record for the
fewest runs produced (66) by a .300 hitter
with enough plate appearances to be a batting title qualifier. Your clue is that two
years later, in his last season, he hit .333 and
had 210 hits and 177 runs produced. Weave
that info into a two-run double.

At-Bats: 15   Hits:
Potential Total Bases: 26   Total Bases:
Potential RBIs: 12   RBIs:

17. Men in Blue

1. He umped in more World Series games (108)
than Mickey Mantle and Roger Maris played
in combined, but never saw either the Mick
or Roger play in a World Series game. Single.

2. He pitched in the first World Series in this
century and thirty years later umped in the
first All-Star game. Two bases.

3. During the early days when an umpire
worked a game all by his lonesome, he stationed himself either behind the pitcher or
behind the catcher, depending on his preference, and rendered all his calls from the
same vantage point for the entire game.
What umpire, later a manager of the Washington National League team, was reputedly

the first to make a practice of working behind the catcher when the bases were empty and then moving behind the pitcher with men on? Two-run homer.

4. He was the first umpire to call balls and strikes in a major league game that his brother played in as a catcher. Double.

5. In August of 1946 this Ohio native, named for another famous Ohioan, became the first graduate of an umpire training school to reach the majors when the AL picked up his contract from the American Association. Two-run homer.

6. Emmett Ashford, in 1966, was the first black arbiter in the AL. Who became the NL's first black ump seven years later? Double.

7. The very first NL game in 1876 was umped by a man who customarily rose at 4:00 A.M. and walked from his Boston home all the way to Providence when he was scheduled to officiate an afternoon contest there. Home run.

8. What happened for the first time in major league history on October 3, 1970, the date of the opening ALCS game between Minnesota and Baltimore? RBI single.

9. As a player he got into only 11 games in the majors, all with Brooklyn in 1902, but ten years later he embarked on a new career that saw him set a major league record for the most consecutive games serving as an ump (3,510), all in the AL. Triple.

10. He's the only player in the HOF who also served for pay as a big league ump—and at that for just part of the 1906 season while he was physically unable to hold down the

Cardinals' first base post. The following year he returned to play 32 more games and make his 2,930th and last hit. RBI single.

11. The only man in both the pro baseball and pro football Halls of Fame is an umpire whose size alone—he was a tackle—commanded utter respect from players. Single.

12. He played with Willie Keeler, managed Charlie Gehringer, and was still umping in the AL when Floyd Giebell beat Bob Feller to clinch the 1940 flag for the Tigers. RBI double.

13. In 1935, his last major league season, this White Sox outfielder was called on to sub for an ailing ump in a game against the Browns. He parlayed the experience into a HOF career as an NL ump, beginning in 1941. RBI single.

14. In 1906, at age 22, he became the youngest full-time ump in history and later was the first ump to write a nationally syndicated sports column. Also a club exec, he's in the HOF and worth a two-bagger.

15. He umped the first AL game in 1901 between Cleveland and Chicago, and 53 years later he was still serving as the junior circuit's first umpire-in-chief. He too is in the HOF and rates a two-bagger.

At-Bats: 15   Hits:
Potential Total Bases: 32   Total Bases:
Potential RBIs: 9   Total RBIs:

18. Wondrous Wildmen

1. He holds the record for the most career walks issued by a southpaw. Single.
2. The only pitcher among the top ten in career walks who is not among the top 100 in career strikeouts issued more walks than he collected K's and ended the career of a HOF catcher when he beaned him. RBI double.
3. His 289 walks in 1890 are an all-time record. Single.
4. Whose record walk total of 274, set only a year earlier, did the above man break in 1890? Two-run homer.
5. His 208 walks in 1938 are the most issued by any hurler since 1900. Single.
6. He set both an AL rookie record and an A's franchise record when he gave up 168 free passes as a frosh in 1916. Home run.
7. He holds both the St. Louis Browns and the original Washington Senators record for the most walks in a season. Two-bagger.
8. He holds both the expansion Washington Senators and the Detroit Tigers record for the most walks in a season. RBI double.
9. In 1955, his first full season in the majors, he set both the 20th-century NL record and a modern Cubs franchise record when he gave up 185 walks. Single.
10. He set the Phillies' 20th-century record when he walked 164 batters in 1911, the year after he topped the NL in strikeouts. More than that I won't tell you. Triple.
11. He won 26 games in 1914 and led NL pitchers in giving up the fewest hits per nine

innings while setting a 20th-century New York Giants record by walking 128 men. Double.

12. He set a rather goofy record in 1941 when he pitched a complete-game shutout despite walking 11 batters. Clues are there for an easy single.

13. His 1,775 career walks, all surrendered while pitching in the AL, are the most given up by a hurler in one league. Single.

14. In 1906 he walked a modern NL record 14 hitters in his lone big league start. Seven years later his elder brother set the all-time NL record when he pitched 68 consecutive innings without walking a man. Just knowing the family name will get you a bingle.

At-Bats: 14   Hits:
Potential Total Bases: 26   Total Bases:
Potential RBIs: 5   RBIs:

19. Silver Sluggers

1. In 1979 what NL slugger hit just one less home run than the entire Houston team? Single, plus an extra base if you know who led the 'stros that year with nine circuit clouts.

2. He was the first catcher to hit 40 or more home runs in a season. Single, and take an RBI if you can nail the year he broke the ice.

3. His 37 homers in his biggest slugging season stood for 23 years as a major league record

for the most four-baggers by a catcher. Two bases.

4. He set a new AL record for catchers when he clubbed 30 four-baggers in 1953. Single.

5. His 17 homers in 1921 set a new AL record for second basemen and broke the old mark of 13, established in 1901 by a Triple Crown winner on the same team. Homer for the record breaker; extra RBI if you get the man whose mark he shattered.

6. His 18 homers in 1926 were both a new major league rookie record and a new AL record for second basemen. RBI double.

7. He tied his own Padres club record in 1972 when he slammed 38 homers, including five in a doubleheader versus the Braves that saw him drive in a record 13 runs. RBI single.

8. Who broke his own club record when he rapped 30 homers for the Blue Jays in 1980 and at that time still held the season home run record for another AL team? Single, plus an extra base for the other team.

9. The last player to post a slugging average above .700 for a full season is also the oldest man ever to top that figure. Single, and an extra base for the year he did it.

10. When Rogers Hornsby walloped 42 homers in 1922, whose 20th century righthanded hitters' season record did he break? Two-bagger, plus an extra base for the year the old mark was set.

11. The only club in either league to hit fewer than 100 four-baggers in homer-happy 1987 nonetheless finished a strong second in its loop in runs scored, thanks largely to the work of what slugger whose 35 homers were

more than a third of his team's total? Need both the team and the player for a single.

12. Never a home run leader, he still succeeded in setting the post-1900 season record to that date for the most home runs by a first baseman when he clouted 19 in 1920. Worth an RBI double if you know this great hitter-for-average who sizzled on one occasion as a slugger too. Take an extra base for knowing who became the new season record holder for first basemen the following year. And grab three more RBIs if you're among the very select few who know what first sacker, back in 1884, hit 21 homers to set a gateway record that stood until 1921.

13. Mel Ott hit his 500th homer off Johnny Hutchings, Ted Williams connected against Wynn Hawkins, and Willie McCovey's 500th victim was Jamie Easterly. Indeed, most 500 club members have hit their monumental homers off lesser-light hurlers. Who's the only club member who hit his historic 500th against a Hall of Fame hurler? Two-bagger, plus an RBI for the hurler.

14. Here's one that will separate the experts from the pretenders. Name all the members of the top ten club in career homers prior to expansion (or at the conclusion of the 1960 season). Grand slam homer if you get 'em all, forget putting them in order—you're too much for me if you can. Double, provided you can nail at least eight of the ten.

At-Bats: 14   Hits:
Potential Total Bases: 28   Total Bases:
Potential RBIs: 13   RBIs:

20. Thieves Like Us

1. What was the last year that neither the AL nor the NL had a black or Latino stolen base champ? It's been a good while, so the year's worth a homer; and you collect an extra RBI for each of the league leaders you can nab from that long ago season.

2. In 1970 he set a new AL record for the highest season stolen base average when he pilfered 33 sacks in 35 tries. It was his first year as a regular, and he proved to be one of the most proficient base thieves of all time. Single.

3. His 401 career steals lead all first basemen. I'll risk the clue that he also holds the season theft record for first sackers and still award an RBI single.

4. He leads all switch hitters in career thefts with 738, which is slightly less than half the number of runs he scored in his 20 years as an NL outfielder. Single.

5. He leads all catchers in career thefts with 176 and at one time held the major league season record for backstoppers as well with 30 steals, set in 1916. Two bases.

6. His 79 thefts are the most in any season since the end of the deadball era by a player of neither black nor Latino extraction. Worth a triple if you can snare this Caucasian flash, plus two RBIs for the year he sped.

7. The last player who was of neither black nor Latino extraction to lead the AL in steals, he was also about the shortest man since Hugh Nicol to be a stolen base champ. Single for

him; two RBIs for the year, which may prove harder.

8. The Cardinals, thanks to Lou Brock and Vince Coleman, have monopolized the NL season stolen base leader charts for the past 25 years. Only three other Cards have ever led the NL in thefts and just one of them did it in consecutive seasons. Name him and score a three-bagger.

9. The last man to steal 60 or more bases in a 154-game season, he did it in 1943 when he snared 61. RBI single.

10. His record for the most season thefts by a second baseman has stood for nearly 80 years. That one clue should set you up for a routine single.

11. No joke now, the name of the man who was the Giants' club leader in 1911, the year that McGraw's men set a 20th-century record with 347 stolen bases, will bring a triple.

12. What was the only team between 1920–41 to feature a trio of outfielders one season who each swiped 20 or more bases? If told the club won a pennant, can you snag it and the year in question for a double? And gee whiz, okay, for pete's sake, I'll credit an RBI for each of its speedy gardeners you can name.

13. Which one of the following former stars ranks as the most proficient base thief in that he had the highest career stolen base average? Single. Luis Aparicio, Amos Otis, Tommy Harper, Lou Brock, Larry Bowa, Mickey Mantle, Jim Landis, Bobby Bonds.

14. A perfect 44-for-44 on the morning of July 29 in a recent season and seemingly a lock to decimate the all-time season stolen base

average record, he fell short of the mark when he was thrown out in ten of his last 27 attempts. Single; RBI for the year he stumbled with the record within his grasp.

15. There are several slewfoots in the Hall of Fame, but none of the following guys really qualifies. Which one of them, do you suppose, swiped the most bases in his career? Double, plus an RBI for knowing which one had the fewest. Stan Musial, Joe DiMaggio, Johnny Mize, Ducky Medwick, Lou Gehrig, Jimmie Foxx, Ted Williams, George Kell, Mel Ott, Hank Greenberg.

At-Bats: 15   Hits:
Potential Total Bases: 25   Total Bases:
Potential RBIs: 14   RBIs:

21. Be It Ever So Humble

1. What club still uses as its home ground a stadium that was originally called Weegham Park? RBI single.

2. For years this team played its weekday games in a place called League Park and used its present home stadium only on weekends and holidays. Two-bagger.

3. What club hosted its first home World Series game in Exposition Park and was ensconced in a new all-concrete and steel stadium that was considered the state of the art at the time when it next appeared in a fall classic?

Two for the team; extra base for its digs in its second Series appearance.

4. Some 50 years after this club's present home park was built in 284 days, the renovation of it took more than twice that long and—of course—cost about a zillion times as much. Single.

5. The name of the first team to have a dome for its home will bring a single, plus an RBI for the year the dome first opened.

6. This team's first home park had the same name as another major league team's park. A lack of imagination? Nope, it was because the park had previously been used by a minor league club whose parent outfit was that other major league team. Two-run double for the club in question and the name of its first home base.

7. Of the eight original AL franchises, all but one still play on real grass in 1991. Which club is the lone defector? Single, and an extra base for its present home.

8. What was the name of the first stadium outside the USA to serve as home to a major league team? Two-bagger.

9. The last new NL stadium to be built without artificial turf, its name and that of the club that calls it home will net you an RBI single.

10. The last year that two major league teams shared the same stadium rates a double—provided you also know the teams, of course.

11. In 1912, a light-hitting first baseman named Hugh Bradley, who never hit another homer in the majors, rapped a historic first four-bagger over what famous outfield wall? Double.

12. Many clubs share a park with a pro football team. What was the last team to play in a stadium that was built expressly to accommodate a pro football outfit? Single, plus an RBI for the name of the park and a second RBI for the pro football crew.

13. Too many easy questions here? I agree. Try this one for size. What team played in a park that had bleachers only in right field that were known as "the jury box"? Two bases for the team; two more bases if you know the year its park first opened—and a grand slam homer if you can also name its old park, which had been in existence prior to its closing for 42 years.

14. What is the only park to serve as home for both an AL and NL pennant winner since World War II? Wager a double I can sneak this one by plenty of you.

At-Bats: 14   Hits:
Potential Total Bases: 26   Total Bases:
Potential RBIs: 8   RBIs:

JULY

The Towering Twosome

It's a rare year nowadays when a batting titlist compiles an average more than 100 points higher than his league's average, but once it was a common occurrence. There was even a season in which two players in the same circuit topped the average hitter in their loop by 140 or more points. How extraordinary a feat is that? Pretty spectacular when you consider that only seven times in this century has a hitter risen as much as 140 points above the rest of the pack in a season. What makes the feat under consideration even more intriguing is that to this day it still hasn't been absolutely and positively established to everyone's satisfaction which of the two men won his league's bat crown that year. Some authorities contend that one of the pair led with a .384 mark while his rival hit .383. Other sources still maintain that the second man rapped .385 and that the .384 hitter's mark is tainted anyway. In any case, the controversy continues to rage, but you're in for a clear-cut double if you know the two great hitters who towered above the average batsman in their league during the season in question—as long as you know the season too, of course!

22. Batting Title Bafflers

1. On several occasions Rogers Hornsby led the NL in both batting and slugging average. Who's the only AL second sacker since the close of the deadball era to do the same? Home run.

2. Rather amazingly, no lefthanded hitters between 1916 and 1950 ever won back-to-back batting crowns in the NL. Who would have accomplished this feat if the current rule for determining a season batting leader had applied throughout the century? Tough but honest triple.

3. According to the rule in effect at the time, he was the lone man to qualify for and win a batting title, only to be denied the crown in favor of a player who was judged more deserving. Two-run homer for him; extra ribby for the actual winner.

4. He was in the majors for 13 years before he had a season in which he batted often enough to qualify for a batting title. Then he hit .321 to finish as the runner-up to the first Padre to cop a bat crown. Double, plus an RBI for the Padre.

5. He lost not only the batting title but also the Triple Crown by a whisker in 1953 when he missed beating out an infield hit in his last at-bat of the season. RBI single.

6. He was a runner-up in both NL and AL batting races before he became the oldest player in NL history to win his first batting crown. Single.

7. The winner of the closest three-way batting

race in history, he would have dropped to third place if he'd gone hitless in just one more at-bat. Two for him; homer if you know all three men involved.

8. The only player since 1893 to be a league leader in batting average one season and pitching strikeouts on another occasion is not named Babe Ruth. Triple.

9. You're on your honor not to give yourself a single if you need longer than ten seconds to name the last first sacker to win a batting crown in the AL.

10. The first shortstop to win a batting crown in a major league other than the old National Association is considered by many authorities to be the best at his position during the last century. Solo homer.

11. He was the first Rookie of the Year Award winner who subsequently won a batting title. Single.

12. Through the 1948 season, he was the only third baseman to win a batting title in *any* major league *anywhere* at *any* time. A must triple for all with a simmering desire to gain that expert's badge.

13. The Pirates have had three shortstops win bat titles but never had a second sacker win one. What's the only team in the majors to have both a shortstop and a second baseman who copped bat crowns? Big clue: you get a single for the team but need three names to score an extra base for snaring all the players involved.

14. Three of the 14 AL teams begin with the letter C. It's the most common letter in the AL—yet just once in the past 35 years has

an AL batting leader played for a team beginning with that letter. Sac hit for the three teams; double for the bat titlist.

At-Bats: 14　　　　　　　Hits:
Potential Total Bases: 36　Total Bases:
Potential RBIs: 8　　　　RBIs:

23. Highway Robbery

Depending on which team claims your allegiance, these trades were some of the best (or worst) ever made.

1. The only reigning home run leader to be traded for a reigning batting champ, he remained a potent slugger for several more seasons while the hitting leader's career batting average declined every year thereafter. Need both for a bingle.
2. Pitcher Bob Kline, shortstop Rabbit Warstler, and $125,000 enticed Connie Mack to dispatch former 20-game winner Rube Walberg, crack leadoff hitter Max Bishop, and what Hall of Fame hurler to the Red Sox in 1933? Single.
3. Maz's presence made a talented frosh second sacker expendable the year the Pirates bagged their first flag in 33 seasons. Three years later Maz's shortstop mate went to the same club that had stripped the Pirates of the second sacker, a move that helped bring

that team its first flag in 18 seasons. Need both men and their team for an RBI single.

4. The Cubs got Doug Clemens and two former 20-game winners for Lou Brock. The pair of ex-20-gamers won a grand total of seven victories in Bruin garb. Name 'em for a triple.

5. Traded for Ray Sadecki, he helped bring his new team two pennants in his three seasons with them. Dealt for Joe Torre in the spring of 1969, he immediately sparked yet another team to the first NL West crown. Single.

6. Rick Wise was all it took to pry this cinch future Hall of Famer from the Cards just prior to the 1972 season. Single.

7. What team got one of the game's top catchers and two future back-to-back Cy Young winners for Sixto Lezcano, David Green, Lary Sorensen, and Dave La Pointe? Name the club and its three acquisitions for a double. Sac hit if you stumble on any part of the package.

8. Pitcher Bob Sykes was all the Yankees got in 1982 for this future batting king and MVP winner. Single.

9. You go to the back of the class if you don't know what future relief ace the Mets packaged with Dan Norman to acquire a fading Ellis Valentine in 1981. Single.

10. Needing a reliable backup to catcher Andy Seminick, the Phils in 1947 handed the Reds a lefty who would become one of the NL's premier pitchers for the next six years in return for Al Lakeman, a career .203 hitter. Being told the portsider twice led the NL in shutouts should get you in for a double.

11. Pirates fans thought their front office

needed medical assistance in late 1975 when this pitcher was all the Bucs got from the Yankees for Willie Randolph, Ken Brett, and Dock Ellis. RBI single.

12. A severe personality clash induced John McGraw to ship what .361 hitter and NL leader in runs scored to the Braves for Shanty Hogan and Jimmy Welsh after the 1927 season? Single.

13. Jack Taylor and his favorite battery mate, Jack O'Neill, went from the Cubs to the Cards in 1902 for what future Hall of Famer and his pet catcher, Larry McLean? Double.

14. In a three-year period from 1969–71 the Royals acquired three players who would form the backbone of their team in the early 1970s for no more than these long-forgotten expendables: John Gelnar, Steve Whitaker, Joe Foy, Jim York, and Lance Clemons. One base for each player the Royals robbed, plus an RBI for nailing the team whose pocket was picked in each instance.

At-Bats: 14   Hits:
Potential Total Bases: 22   Total Bases:
Potential RBIs: 5   RBIs:

24. The Magic Circle

1. The lone Expos hurler to win 20 games, he cracked the magic circle for the only time in his career in 1978. Double.

2. What was the only team during the 1980s

with two 20-game winners that failed to make it to the World Series? Single.

3. Dave Stewart was the only hurler during the 1980s to be a 20-game winner for three consecutive seasons. Who was the only NL pitcher during the 1980s to make the 20-game circle in consecutive years? Single.

4. The period between 1946–55 is considered by many to be the greatest decade in major league history. Who was the only NL southpaw besides Warren Spahn to win 20 or more games twice during that span? Two-bagger.

5. The last righthander to win 20 games in a season while wearing a Philadelphia A's uniform had been out of the game for more than 15 years when the A's deserted Philly. Who was he for two bases?

6. The only Yankees pitcher since 1920 to win 20 games more than once without ever copping 20 for a pennant-winning team reached the magic circle three times for Bronx also-ran outfits. Single.

7. He and Joe Wood are the only 30-game winners in this century who never again won 20 in a campaign after their magic seasons. RBI double.

8. A record ten AL pitchers won 20 or more games in 1971, including four for Baltimore alone. The only AL hurler to lose 20 or more games that year had earlier been the last pitcher since 1935 to perform a much more famous feat. Must have both him and his feat to earn a single.

9. In 1892 there were 22 pitchers in the NL (some books say 23) who won 20 or more

games and at least one on each of the 12 teams. Who was the lone 20-game winner for that year's cellar dweller? You'll be blue if you don't use the clue that two years later, still in the same garb, he won 25 games for a pennant winner. Two-run triple.

10. The first pitcher to win 20 games for an AL basement dweller did it in the war-abbreviated 1918 season when the schedule ended on Labor Day. Two-bagger.

11. The first pitcher to win 20 games for a Yankees pennant winner and the last pitcher to win 20 games for a Red Sox team that won a World Championship are one and the same man. RBI single.

12. The Yankees dynasty from 1936–39 had five 20-game winners, but only two Yankees pitchers made the magic circle. One won 20 all four years, the other only in 1936. Need both for a single.

13. The Yankees dynasty from 1949–53 had at least one 20-game winner every year but one. That season an ex-Yankee led the AL with 22 wins. He's a double; the year goes for an RBI.

14. He was the lone NL hurler to win 20 games more than once during the six-year span between 1928–33, considered to be the greatest period for hitting in NL history. Take a triple.

At-Bats: 14   Hits:
Potential Total Bases: 23   Total Bases:
Potential RBIs: 5   RBIs:

25. Jack of all Trades

1. Tony Phillips tied a record when he played three different positions in the 1989 World Series. The first player to do what Tony did is in the Hall of Fame and led the NL in RBIs the year he was seen at three different stations in a Series. Want more? The following season he became one of the tallest men ever to be a regular second baseman when he was moved there temporarily to make room for another Hall of Famer. And the man whose spot he took at second? Well, he split that year about equally among second, short, and third and is in the HOF too. Name all three of these Famers for a triple; zip for less.

2. The only player in history to be a regular at five different positions, he held down every spot on the diamond except pitcher, catcher, short, and center field. Single.

3. The first post-1893 player to be a regular at various times for the same club as a second baseman, shortstop, and third sacker was replaced by Joe Tinker when he jumped to the St. Louis Browns in 1902. Two-run homer.

4. Nobody ever played 1,000 or more games at two different positions without one of his homes being first base. He came the closest when he got into 1,078 games in the outfield and 955 as a third sacker. One more clue: he was the first to participate in two World Series as a regular at two different positions. Double.

5. The only catcher also to be a regular at two

other positions, he had 100-RBI seasons while playing all three positions. Single.

6. He led the AL in steals as a third baseman and batting as a second baseman—and one year had the poorest fielding average of all AL shortstops. Double.

7. He was voted Rookie of the Year as a third baseman, led the AL in fielding average as a second baseman, and topped the AL one year in double plays by a shortstop. On all three occasions he played in a World Series. RBI single.

8. He holds the record for the most home runs in a season by a shortstop and shares the mark for the most total chances in a game by a first baseman. Single.

9. The career record holder for the fewest double plays grounded into by any player active ten or more seasons played second base for Al Lopez, third base for Eddie Stanky, and the outfield for Earl Weaver. Double.

10. The first man to be selected as an All-Star game starter in both leagues won Rookie of the Year honors as a third baseman, an MVP Award as a first baseman, and fanned a then NL-record 161 times in his only year as a regular outfielder. Single.

11. Playing second in 1937, he was the hardest rookie in the NL to fan. At shortstop in 1938, he led the NL in at-bats. As a third sacker in 1941, he had his best year at the plate—.306—and finished fourth in the MVP vote. A homer for a guy who may have been the NL's best all-around infielder back then.

12. He hit .229 as a rookie shortstop, holds the

record for the most consecutive errorless chances by a third baseman, and had his top home run (25) and RBI (83) year while playing second base. RBI single.

13. He won two batting crowns, one as a second sacker and one at first base, and played shortstop on the last Washington Senators team managed by Bucky Harris. Single.

14. Not a name that comes readily to mind when you think of versatile players, he nonetheless won a batting crown as a rookie second baseman, fielded .806 in his only year as a regular at the hot corner, and committed 44 errors to give him a .791 fielding average as a center fielder in 1886. For pete's sake, please don't miss this two-bagger.

At-Bats: 14   Hits:
Potential Total Bases: 27   Total Bases:
Potential RBIs: 5   RBIs:

26. Their Niche Is Secure

1. He's the only infielder since 1900 (first basemen included) to register a season on-base percentage of over .500. Single, plus an RBI for the year he did it.

2. Who were the last two players to achieve a season on-base percentage of .500 or better? Single, and an RBI for the year both did it.

3. His .488 on-base percentage in his best season is the highest since expansion began. It was the first year he made enough plate

appearances to be a batting title qualifier, and in his second-best season, which came two years later, his OBP was exactly 100 points lower. Two-run single.

4. He has the NL's highest season on-base percentage (.471) since expansion occurred. Your big clue is he combined a career-high .327 batting average with a career-high 132 walks the year he did it. Single.

5. He holds the all-time season record (301) for runs produced—runs scored + RBIs—home runs—and set a loop season RBI record the year he did it. Single; extra base for the year.

6. He set a modern NL record for runs produced (288) during a season in which he failed to lead the senior circuit in *either* runs or RBIs. Single, plus an RBI for the year he did it.

7. He is the lone player since World War II to have a season that ranks among the all-time top 25 in runs produced. Single, plus two RBIs for his big year.

8. Only one pitcher during the 1980s toiled more than 300 innings in a season. He's a single and the year he became perhaps the last ever to do what he did rates an RBI.

9. The last time a pitcher in the AL worked over 300 innings in a season was 1977 when two did it. Name either for a single; RBI double for both.

10. Excepting the strike-shortened 1981 season, he was the lone hurler to post an ERA below 2.00 in the 1980s. Single; extra base for the year.

11. The holder of the AL record for the most

shutouts in a season (13) that same year became the only AL hurler ever to win three games in a five-game World Series. Need both him and his glory year for a two-bagger.

12. Who are the only two players in history who averaged .400+ over a span of four consecutive seasons? One did it actually over a five-year span, and you need both for a single.

13. He hit .433 in 1925 with 42 hits and 20 RBIs, the highest batting average ever by a pitcher making 100 or more plate appearances in a season. Telling you that he also won 20 games for a pennant winner that year should make this about your easiest single in the book.

14. He threw the last pitch in the first AL pennant playoff game and the last pitch in the final World Series game played in the home park of the first franchise to move since 1903. Both events occurred less than two weeks apart—and in the same city! Deuce for him; RBI for the city.

At-Bats: 14   Hits:
Potential Total Bases: 19   Total Bases:
Potential RBIs: 10   RBIs:

27. Great Glovemen

1. In 1965, five years after winning a Gold Glove at another position, he amassed, 1,682 putouts, the most in a season by any first baseman since 1926. Single.

2. Andre Dawson and Gary Carter both won Gold Gloves in 1980. Each subsequently won several more, but the only two Expos prior to 1980 to win Gold Gloves each took just one. Homer for both; single if you know just one of them.

3. No member of the expansion Washington Senators ever won a Gold Glove. He was the only original Senators player to win one. RBI triple.

4. An outstanding all-around performer, deft enough to play every infield position and also in the outfield when not on the mound, he set an all-time season record for *any* player at *any* position when he averaged 4.68 assists per game in 1905 while leading the St. Louis Browns in wins and ERA. Two-run homer.

5. He set the all-time record for catchers in 1916 when he participated in 36 double plays but was involved in only one twin-killing four years later while backstopping for the World Champs. RBI triple.

6. He's the lone member on the top ten list of season leaders in putouts by a third baseman who played after the deadball era ended. Moreover, he holds the AL season record with 243 putouts, a figure that shattered his own mark of 235, which was set the previous year. Two-bagger.

7. The first player at any position to field a perfect 1.000 while participating in over 100 games did it for a cellar team that finished with a .278 winning percentage and the NL's poorest fielding average. After being told that he also led his club in homers (9),

RBIs (56), and batting (.271), and that Nick Etten was the runner-up to him in all three departments, all your burners should be lit. RBI double, plus an extra base for his dismal team.

8. He was the first (and to date the only) first baseman ever to post a perfect 1.000 fielding average for a full season. One, plus an RBI for his flawless year.

9. In 1937 he came within a single point of the NL record at his position when he fielded .982. No NL'er since has come so close to the circuit's all-time top mark. He rates a homer, but take a sac hit if you know only the position he played.

10. One of many early-day players whose fielding kept them in the game, he averaged an all-time record 13.3 chances per game at first base for Louisville in 1876. A year later he set a record (since broken) for the most chances per game by a second baseman, and in 1885 he set the all-time record for the lowest season batting average by a second sacker when he hit .155 for the New York Giants. Three-run homer.

11. Lou Boudreau and he are the only two men on the list for the top ten career fielding averages by a shortstop who finished their major league careers prior to the beginning of the free agency era in 1976. Three-bagger.

12. He shattered the all-time mark for shortstops when he garnered 621 assists 56 years after Glenn Wright set the old mark with 601. Single, plus an extra base for the year the new record was established.

At-Bats: 12   Hits:
Potential Total Bases: 32   Total Bases:
Potential RBIs: 11   RBIs:

28. Ryan Rousers

1. Excluding pitchers, who are the only two Hall of Famers who were active after 1968 whom Nolan Ryan failed to fan at least once? Double for both; one'll get you a sac hit.

2. Ryan has fanned each member of two trios of brothers. Should be a snap single once you know the Allens weren't one of the trios.

3. Several father and son combos have both fallen prey to Ryan's heaters. Who were the first pair to both be fanned by him? Double.

4. When Ryan fanned 383 hitters in 1973, whose post-1893 record did he break? Single.

5. Ryan has K'd 300 or more hitters a record six times. Who is the only other AL hurler to fan that many in a season more than once? RBI single.

6. What one-time National League Championship Series MVP homered off Ryan in his first major league at-bat and was subsequently fanned 12 times by him in his first three seasons? Single.

7. Break the string and rack up a double by naming which one of the following players has been Ryan's most frequent K victim. Reggie Jackson, Rod Carew, Darryl Straw-

berry, Claudell Washington, Jorge Orta, Darrell Porter, Dale Murphy, Mike Schmidt.

8. Ryan has K'd at least two men whose last names begin with every letter of the alphabet except X. The letter Q is represented by exactly two victims. One is Jamie Quirk; collect a homer for the other after being told his father was a major league pitcher and his mother's maiden name was Goldie Bowersox.

9. Ryan's historic 5,000th K victim has already carved a sizable niche in the record books in his own right. You, however, have just an empty space in your column if you don't single here.

10. Nolan set a new record in 1987 when he averaged 11.46 strikeouts per nine innings. What fireballer's old mark of 11.39 did he break? RBI single.

11. What was the only year between 1972 and 1979 that Ryan, owing partly to arm trouble, failed to average at least nine K's per every nine innings? Single.

12. Ryan has appeared in just one World Series. When was it? Single.

13. Despite usually pitching a large number of innings. Nolan has been tagged on just one occasion for as many as 20 homers in a season. Need both the year and his team at the time for a triple.

14. What was the last year prior to 1989 that Ryan fanned 300 or more batters? Single.

15. Ryan's total number of walks through 1989 (2,540) were more than the number of career strikeouts that all but one of the following Hall of Fame fireballers achieved. Single.

Don Drysdale, Lefty Grove, Dazzy Vance, Rube Waddell, Amos Rusie, Bob Feller, Sandy Koufax.

At-Bats: 15   Hits:
Potential Total Bases: 23   Total Bases:
Potential RBIs: 3   RBIs:

AUGUST

The Sweet Sixteen

Below is a chronological chart of 16 games.

NO.	Date	Opponent	Losing Pitcher	Park	Score
1	April 18	Boston	Dick Rudolph	Baker Bowl	4–0
2	May 3	Boston	Pat Ragan	Braves Field	3–0
3	May 13	Cincinnati	Gene Dale	Redlands Field	5–0
4	May 18	Pittsburgh	Erv Kantlehner	Forbes Field	3–0
5	May 26	Brooklyn	Sherry Smith	Baker Bowl	1–0
6	June 3	St. Louis	Lee Meadows	Baker Bowl	2–0
7	July 7	St. Louis	Lee Meadows	Robison Field	1–0
8	July 15	Pittsburgh	Elmer Jacobs	Forbes Field	4–0
9	July 20	Cincinnati	Fred Toney	Redlands Field	6–0
10	August 2	Chicago	Mike Prendergast	Baker Bowl	1–0*
11	August 9	Cincinnati	Al Schulz	Baker Bowl	1–0
12	August 14	New York	Rube Benton	Baker Bowl	8–0
13	August 18	Cincinnati	Al Schulz	Redlands Field	3–0
14	Sept. 1	Brooklyn	Jack Coombs	Baker Bowl	3–0
15	Sept. 23	Cincinnati	Fred Toney	Baker Bowl	4–0
16	Oct. 2	Boston	Pat Ragan	Baker Bowl	2–0

*In 12 innings

After I add that all 16 games occurred in the same season and that a certain pitcher was involved in each of the 16 contests, can you score an RBI single by pinning down both his name and the year he did what no other pitcher before or since has ever done?

29. Home Run Leaders

1. He was the first righthanded hitter whose home base was Fenway Park to lead the AL in homers. Single, plus two RBIs for the year he first did it.
2. The first White Sox player to hit more than 35 homers in a season, he led the AL twice. Single.
3. Prior to Ralph Kiner's arrival, how long had it been since the Pirates had had the NL's top home run hitter and who was he? Triple for the player; three ribbies if you nail the exact time span.
4. The first player whose home park was Griffith Stadium to lead the AL in homers was not Harmon Killebrew or Goose Goslin. Take two bases for him and an RBI for the year he put Washington on the four-bagger chart.
5. Who was the first Phillies player to lead the NL in homers while playing in a home park other than the Baker Bowl? Single, plus an RBI for the year it first happened.
6. His 24 homers for Brooklyn led the NL one year and stood as a record for first basemen until Lou Gehrig broke it in 1927. Double for him; RBI for the year he topped the senior loop.
7. Which one of the following sluggers of the 1940s and 1950s was never a league home run leader? Single. Rudy York, Gus Zernial, Del Ennis, Larry Doby, Ted Kluzewski, Rocky Colavito, Hank Sauer, Eddie Mathews, Dolf Camilli.

8. Between 1931 and 1945 only two right-handed hitters led the NL in homers. One won the crown outright and the other shared it, but you need both to score an RBI double.

9. Who was the only league home run leader in this century, Ted Williams, 1942, excepted, who didn't play a single game in the majors the following year? Gigantic clue: he was the first 20th-century home run leader to later win a pennant as a player-manager. Triple.

10. The first member of a St. Louis team to lead the NL in homers, he set a new loop record when he did it. He rates just a single, but his record figure and the year he achieved it will get two RBIs.

11. Of the four NL expansion teams, only the Mets have had a league home run leader. Naming him will earn you just a sac hit, but you can snag a two-bagger if you know which of the eight NL franchises in existence prior to expansion hasn't had a home run leader for over 30 years now—as long as you also know who was its last champ!

12. What team had the first AL home run king and also the most different home run leaders (7) prior to 1953 when the first franchise move since 1903 occurred? Single for the team; two-run homer if, in addition, you know all seven of its champs.

13. No switch-sticker has ever won an NL home run crown outright and just one has tied for the top spot. You're on a two-base tear if you know him.

14. The oldest player to win an AL home run crown was also the first player from his team

to be a reigning four-bagger champ in nearly 40 years. He'll bring a single; the man who was the club's last champ before him rates an extra base.

15. End on a high note by naming the youngest man ever to win a league home run crown. Single, plus an RBI for the year he led.

At-Bats: 15   Hits:
Potential Total Bases: 28   Total Bases:
Potential RBIs: 14   RBIs:

30. Contact Was Their Middle Name

1. Three years before Joe Sewell broke his major league mark by fanning just four times in 1925, this shortstop set a new record when he whiffed only five times. Still the holder of the NL season record for the most at-bats per strikeout (118.4), he's going for a two-run triple.

2. He's the only player active exclusively since expansion began in 1961 to average as many as 24 career at-bats per strikeout. Very quietly, almost unnoticed, he collected 1,617 hits during a 14-year career. In, 5,791 at-bats he fanned just 242 times, but one of his flaws was he never walked much either. Top year was 1970 when he scored an even 100 runs and hit .310. RBI triple.

3. Between 1925 and 1933, Joe Sewell led the AL every year in fewest strikeouts. Upon his

retirement, another Joe assumed his crown in 1934 by fanning just 10 times while stroking .341. Double.

4. Who are the only two members of the 500 home run club who had fewer than 1,000 career strikeouts? Need both for a single.

5. Only two catchers with over 400 official at-bats have ever led their league in fewest strikeouts. Both played for the same team the seasons they did it and both are in the Hall of Fame—and, of course, you need both for a single.

6. He led the AL a record ten seasons in fewest strikeouts, the last time in 1963. Moreover, he also led the NL once. Single.

7. He was the last player to hit .350+ while topping his league in fewest strikeouts. Even after telling you he copped an MVP Award that year, I'll still credit a homer.

8. The hardest catcher in history to fan, he went down on strikes just 217 times in 5,169 career at-bats and never more than 25 times in a season. RBI single.

9. He finished his career with 1,310 more walks than strikeouts, by far the largest differential of any player in the Hall of Fame. Single.

10. Mickey Mantle leads all switch hitters in career strikeouts. What great second sacker was the hardest switch hitter to fan? Double.

11. After leading the NL three times in fewest strikeouts, he joined the Red Sox in 1982 and promptly topped the AL in the same department. Single.

12. He once hit 51 homers while fanning just 42

times. Single, but you also need the year he became the only 50-homer guy to collect fewer than 50 whiffs.

13. Between 1953 and 1956, he slugged 171 homers, an average of nearly 43 per season, while averaging just 37 K's per season. RBI single if you bag the right clue here.

14. The most difficult righthanded hitter in history to fan, he K'd just 189 times in 6,667 career at-bats between 1913 (when batter's K's were first recorded by the AL) and 1927, including a record low for first basemen of only five in 1921. Two-bagger.

15. He hammered 361 career homers while fanning just 369 times, far and away the smallest differential among men with 300+ home runs. Single.

At-Bats: 15
Potential Total Bases: 25
Potential RBIs: 6

Hits:
Total Bases:
RBIs:

31. Fabled Free Swingers

Now that you've got your mind in that contact groove, let's see how quickly you can give it a 180-degree turn.

1. Only two members of the top ten in career batters' strikeouts were active prior to the first wave of expansion in 1961. Need both to score a single.

2. In 1986 three AL frosh players broke George

Scott's old AL rookie record of 152 K's. One shattered the all-time yearling mark by fanning 185 times. For a single, name both him and the man whose record he broke. Take two more bases if you know the other two AL rookies who topped the old loop mark in 1986.

3. Fourth on the all-time career list with 1,869 K's, he never led either league in strikeouts although he played in both. Single.

4. He set a new AL record when he sawed the air 186 times in just 474 at-bats in 1987. Single.

5. Through 1989, the above man has averaged 36.3 K's per 100 at-bats, second on the all-time list among players with over 1,500 career at-bats to only what fabled free-swinger from the 1960s? Two-bagger.

6. Sandy Koufax K'd 386 times in 776 career at-bats for a .497 K average. What backup catcher with an equally apt last initial began the 1990 season with a .430 K average after whiffing 163 times in his first 379 career at-bats? Double.

7. Which of the following sluggers is the only one who managed to win a home run crown while fanning less than 100 times that same season? Single. Gorman Thomas, Dale Murphy, Dick Allen, Reggie Jackson, Willie Stargell, George Foster, Tony Armas, Jim Rice.

8. No player who spent his entire career at shortstop has ever fanned over 1,000 times. But two who began as shortstops before moving to other positions have done it. One is Ernie Banks; take an RBI single if you snag the other.

9. Reggie Jackson holds a multitude of season and career strikeout records. Among them are how many season franchise K marks? Single.

10. Just three times in history has a player fanned 150 or more times in a season and somehow still managed to hit .300 or better. Who holds the record for the most K's (153) among the trio who have performed this rarity? Even the clue that he set the mark in 1988 may not be enough for some of you to double here.

11. Which of the following pre-1980 sluggers is the only one who either fanned 100 times in a season or was a league leader in K's? Single. Roger Maris, Gil Hodges, Hank Aaron, Billy Williams, Lou Gehrig, Cy Williams, Rocky Colavito, Duke Snider.

12. In 1963 an AL outfielder broke the old ML season K record when he fanned 151 times in his first year as a regular. You won't find his name in any record books, however, because another AL outfielder that same season fanned 175 times in his *only* year as a regular. The experts will nail both wild swingers for a home run; others of you may need a key to get into this house.

13. Which of the following free swingers is the only one to fan less than 100 times during a season in which he had enough plate appearances to be a batting title qualifier? Single. Dick Stuart, Nate Colbert, Frank Howard, Bobby Bonds, Dave Kingman, Cory Snyder, Jose Canseco, Jesse Barfield, Bobby Darwin.

At-Bats: 13⁻ Hits:
Potential Total Bases: 21 Total Bases:
Potential RBIs: 2 RBIs:

32. Team Teasers

1. What team still has an all-time winning percentage above .500 even though it's had only six winning seasons in the past 30 years? Must have been an early-day powerhouse, you're thinking. No, actually it was just at one time a consistently good team that could never quite become a great one. Single.

2. This proud team claimed no connection with the club that later bore its name—and for good reason. It topped its circuit with an overall .641 winning percentage for the ten years the loop existed as a rival major league to the NL. RBI single for the team and the league it dominated.

3. Just twice in this team's 90-year history has it had a player who led its league in total bases. The pair did it 38 years apart—and it's been 37 years since the last man accomplished it. Math will get you the years it occurred, but you need to know your oats to corral the team and both its total base champs in order to net a two-run double.

4. The same year this team swept a record 20 doubleheaders en route to a pennant, it lost 16 games to the Cardinals, the most losses ever by a flag winner to an also-ran. Experts won't need any more clues to score a bingle, but others may like to know that the club led the NL in complete games that year and its top winner was Hank Wyse.

5. What team tumbled into the cellar for the first time in its 52-year history in large part because it was 9–35 in doubleheader action and the only club ever to play 20 or more

twin bills in a season without sweeping at least one? Double.

6. This AL team beat Baltimore the first time in history the two clubs met, then lost the next 23 games the pair played, setting an all-time record for the most consecutive losses to one team. For the savvy, all but one AL team will be swiftly eliminated and the answer will be obvious. Single.

7. The worst fielding team since 1901 was on display in 1904 when this club had a .936 fielding average. If told that it nevertheless had a loop fielding leader in Harry Wolverton, whose FA that year was by far the best of any NL hot corner man, name that club for a deuce.

8. Consistently the best fielding team in the majors since 1900, this club has led its league in fewest errors 19 times in this century and holds its loop's record for the highest fielding average in both a 154- and a 162-game season. RBI single.

9. The only team ever to turn 200 or more double plays three years in a row, the middle of its infield was manned by Pete Suder and Eddie Joost. Single for the club; extra base for the years its keystoners shone.

10. The Orioles matched the biggest gain in history from the previous year by a club that failed to win either a pennant or a division title when they jumped 32½ games in 1989 over their 1988 mark. Whose record did they match? Big hint: Casey Stengel piloted the club the season it improved so dramatically. Two-bagger.

11. In 1920 the White Sox had four 20-game

winners but finished second. What's the only NL team since 1920 to fail to win at least a division title despite having three 20-game winners? Your clues are the trio were caught by Bubbles Hargrave, and the club came in second but didn't finish that high again for 16 years. RBI double.

12. After trading a Hall of Fame hurler, this team went a record 32 seasons without having a 20-game winner. Learning that another Hall of Famer broke the dry spell by bagging 20 should enable you to snatch a single for the team, plus an RBI for the two Famers and a second RBI for the exact years of the team's 20-game drought.

13. What team had at least one 20-game winner for a record 13 consecutive seasons? All you should need is the clue that it had a 25-game winner who copped the Cy Young in the last year of its streak. Single, plus an RBI for the Cy Younger.

14. The only team since expansion to hold opponents to fewer than three runs per game (472 in 162 games) scored just 583 runs itself but won the pennant. The year this happened will be nearly as obvious to most historians as the team, so you need the total package for a single.

15. What team holds the all-time record for vaulting the most positions in the standings from the previous year? All the help you'll get is that the team played in what at the time was a 12-club circuit. Triple.

At-Bats: 15   Hits:
Potential Total Bases: 23   Total Bases:
Potential RBIs: 8   RBIs:

33. Shell-Shocked Slingers

1. He's the lone slinger in history to serve up a gopher ball to four consecutive batters. With the Angels at the time, he was taken deep in a 1963 game by a quartet who had just 35 combined homers that year: Woodie Held, Pete Ramos, Tito Francona, and Larry Brown. It was his last full season after nearly a decade as one of Detroit's better starters. Two bases, plus an extra base for knowing the team that hammered him.

2. He set the season record for the most homers surrendered to one club when the Yankees hit 15 taters off him in 1960. Notwithstanding his kindness to the Bombers, he topped the AL in wins that year. RBI single.

3. The last pitcher to surrender six homers in a game, he was also tagged for a record 22 total bases by Red Sox hitters in the sixth inning of that contest. It occurred in 1940, and he led the AL in losses that year. RBI double.

4. In his only big league game he was pounded for a record 24 runs but nevertheless went the route. The reason: he was the lone pitcher his club had in uniform that day. How come? Well, if I tell you it happened on May 18, 1912, the victors were the A's, the shell-shocked hurler was later a priest in the Philly area, and the losers played such ancients as Hughey Jennings and Deacon McGuire in that game, maybe you can figure out for a single what occasioned this hurler's

only day in big league raiment. Two-run homer for his name.

5. In his last season this 285-game winner gave up an all-time record most runs in one inning when 16 Boston Beareaters crossed the plate in the first frame on June 18, 1894. Traded shortly thereafter by the Orioles, he went to Cleveland in return for John Clarkson. RBI double.

6. He won 12 of his team's 17 victories in 1883, making him its ace. But what an ace! He lost an all-time record 48 games and also gave up an all-time record 549 runs. Even casual historians should bag an easy homer here.

7. His 3.80 career ERA is the highest of any pitcher in the Hall of Fame. To boot, he also holds the AL record for the most career runs surrendered (2,117). Single.

8. The 20th-century record holder for the most earned runs allowed in a season—186 in 1938—still won 20 games somehow for a seventh place team that year. Two bases for him; RBI for his team.

9. In 1930 he posted a 6.20 ERA, the worst ever for a pitcher in 200 or more innings, when he gave up a post-1901 NL record 155 earned runs. Learning that he still managed to have a winning season (15–10) should tell you this guy pitched for a pretty fair-hitting team that year. RBI double; extra RBI for his team.

10. Pitching in relief versus Cleveland on June 10, 1932, he was raked for 29 hits, the most allowed in a game by any pitcher—starter or reliever—since 1901. But he got the win when his club scored its 18th run in the

18th inning. RBI single; extra base for his team.

11. He gave up a post-1893 record 415 hits and 224 runs for the 1900 Giants. His ERA was still a semi-respectable 3.53 as he won 19 games and led the NL in starts. Two-run homer.

12. What vaunted Phils' bonus baby in 1948 set a 20th-century NL record when he was shelled for 18 total bases in a single inning? Toledo fans, who'll remember him as one of the Mud Hens' mound mainstays in the mid-1950s, ought to score a quick grand slam; most of the rest of you will probably bicker with me over the sketchy clues I've given.

13. He holds the all-time career records for both the most homers allowed and the most times being a league leader in hits allowed. Withal, he's in the Hall of Fame. Single.

At-Bats: 13   Hits:
Potential Total Bases: 33   Total Bases:
Potential RBIs: 16   RBIs:

34. Managerial Musings

1. Has there ever been a World Series between two teams that were both managed by men who never played in the majors? If so, when? RBI single.

2. Who was the most recent manager without major league playing experience to win a

World Series with an NL team? Look sharp
for the clue here and collect two bases.

3. In 1955 the AL began the season with a then
record six new managers. What were the
only two teams to keep the same skippers
who'd led them on Opening Day in 1954 and
who were the two retainees? Need the bun-
dle for a single.

4. Which one of the following skippers never
managed Brooklyn to an NL pennant? Single. Walter Alston, Ned Hanlon, Wilbert
Robinson, Burt Shotton, Monte Ward, Leo
Durocher, Bill McGunnigle.

5. Who is the only man who won an MVP
Award after World War II and *later* in his
life won a flag as a manager? Single.

6. He's the only pitcher to win 200 or more
games in this century and also manage a
World Champion. Single, plus an RBI for
the year he triumphed.

7. Who is the only batting-title winner to manage an NL flag winner while no longer an
active player? Double.

8. He's the only flag-winning manager who hit
300 or more career home runs. Single.

9. By a one-year margin, he earned the distinction of being the first manager to win a flag
in the 20th century without ever having
been a major league player. Three for him;
two RBIs for the man he beat out for the
honor by a year.

10. He was the first man in this century to play
on a World Series winner and later manage
one—two actually! RBI double, plus two
more RBIs for the three years in question.

11. Among managers who've piloted at least one

flag winner, he holds the record for playing the most seasons without ever being on a pennant winner. Two-bagger.

12. Freddie Hutchinson, Tom LaSorda, Roger Craig, and Dallas Green are four of the five ex-big league pitchers to manage an NL flag winner since the close of World War II. Name the fifth for a triple.

13. Who holds the record for the most pennants won by an ex-big league first baseman? The only clue you receive is he's in the Hall of Fame. Double.

14. Connie Mack managed the A's for a record 19 consecutive seasons without a flag at one juncture. What manager retained his job for the second-longest pennantless span? Your hints are that he once played for Mack and later managed a rival AL also-ran while Mack was still in the throes of his long drought. Two-bagger.

At-Bats: 14   Hits:
Potential Total Bases: 24   Total Bases:
Potential RBIs: 6   RBIs:

35. Their Niche Is Secure

1. Rogers Hornsby was the first second baseman to club 250+ career home runs. Who was the first AL second sacker to top the 250 mark? RBI single.

2. His 277 homers are the most anyone in his-

tory has hit while playing as a shortstop. Single.

3. Mickey Mantle leads all switch hitters in career homers by a huge margin. Who is a distant second to the Mick? Single.

4. He was the first black player to slug 250+ homers in his career. Two-bagger.

5. His record for the most career pinch homers (11) stood for 31 years until it was broken in 1960. Double for the guy who had 11; two extra bases for the guy who broke his record; plus an RBI if you know the current record holder.

6. He's 16th in career losses with 230 and the lone pitcher in the 20th century to lose 200 games and fail to win 200. RBI single.

7. When Murray Dickson gave up 39 homers in 1948, he became only the second pitcher in history to do something that's now relatively common—surrender 35 or more homers in a season. The first to do it was taken deep exactly 35 times in the same year that a teammate of his set a season record (albeit disputed) for home runs that stood until Babe Ruth broke it in 1919. Single for the hurler; extra base for his slugging teammate; sac hit for knowing just the year in question.

8. The last Cubs pitcher to notch 30 complete games in a season was also the last Bruin to lead the NL in that department. Single.

9. Who is the only black or Latino hurler to win 250 or more games in his career? Single.

10. In 1930, Hack Wilson set the NL home run record with 56. Ralph Kiner and Johnny Mize threatened the mark in 1947 before finishing with 51 apiece. Who was the only

NL player between 1930 and 1947 to club 40 or more homers in a season? Your clue is that when he did it he also became the last member of a certain NL team to lead the senior circuit in homers. Double, plus an RBI for the team.

11. After Frank Howard banged 44 taters in 1970, eight years passed before another AL slugger topped the 40 mark. Who broke the drought in 1978? Single.

12. He hit 77 career homers, the most by any catcher active exclusively prior to 1920— and still the most by any backstopper who labored with his mitt worn on his right hand. Two-bagger.

13. He was the only player active prior to 1900 to average more than two home runs per 100 at-bats. Triple.

14. He was the only lefty hitter who hit all his career four-baggers in the NL to average over six homers per 100 at-bats. RBI single.

15. In 1921, the same season that Babe Ruth broke Roger Connor's career home run record with his 138th homer, he also broke whose 20th-century career record of 119 homers? Double.

At-Bats: 15   Hits:
Potential Total Bases: 24   Total Bases:
Potential RBIs: 3   RBIs:

SEPTEMBER

The Badly Battered Bird

One year a certain righthander toiled for a team that surrendered a record 226 home runs. All by himself he gave up 31 gopher balls in just 105 innings and rang up a dismal 6.43 ERA. His last major league start came in a game that saw the Blue Jays hit a record 10 home runs. That same day a teammate of his was lifted late in the one-sided contest to end an all-time record skein. The team the beleaguered righty worked for rates only a sacrifice hit. His record-setting teammate will earn a single, provided you're targeted on what the streak he had going was. The pitcher, however, is worth two RBIs.

36. Fabulous Keystone Combos

1. What was the first shortstop and second base pair who played in the majors as teammates to make the Hall of Fame? Single.
2. Four other keystone combos have made the Hall of Fame. Which of the four played the most seasons beside each other? RBI single.
3. Who is the only second baseman in the Hall of Fame who played beside two Hall of Fame shortstops during his career? Single, plus an extra base for the pair of shortstops.
4. The only Hall of Fame shortstop who played beside two Hall of Fame second sackers did

it in consecutive seasons. May prove a rugged double, so I'll give an RBI for the second sackers, who'll both be a snap once you stumble on the shortstop.

5. The first keystone combo in this century to play beside each other in over 100 games and both lead their league in fielding average played for a Windy City club, but neither is in the Hall of Fame. Triple for the pair; extra base for the year they both topped their circuit in FA.

6. The first keystone combo in this century to play beside each other in over 100 games and both lead their league in fielding average two consecutive seasons featured a Hall of Famer and a great glove artist who also later topped his league in fielding at another position. Neither man ever played on a pennant winner. Single for one; triple for both; two RBIs for the back-to-back years they led.

7. Who was the first keystone pair to both win Gold Gloves in the same year? Two, plus an RBI for the year.

8. He's the only Gold Glove shortstop to date who played beside two Gold Glove second basemen. Single, and an extra base for the second sackers.

9. What was the first expansion team to feature a Gold Glove keystone combo and who were the combo? Need it all for an RBI double.

10. Who was the only keystone combo to each win consecutive Gold Gloves while playing on a team that won consecutive World Championships? RBI single.

11. The only year a player with the top career fielding average in history at one of the two

keystone positions won a Gold Glove, he played beside a fellow Gold Glover. Single, plus an RBI for his partner.

12. They were the most recent keystone combo each to win back-to-back Gold Gloves. Single.

13. The first keystone combo to both lead their league in fielding showcased the first key-stoner to win an NL batting crown and a shortstop who was the circuit's third-best hitter that year. Single for the bat titlist; triple for both.

14. Boston and Baltimore dominated the NL in the early to mid-1890s, but neither had the NL's top keystone combo of that period. For what team did this pair play from 1891 through 1896 and who were they? One member is considered the best fielder at his position in the last century, if not ever, and the other was the lone member of the 1884 Altoona Union Association club who went on to become a big league standout. Single for one; homer for both.

15. In 1878, when George Wright fielded .947, an average that stood as a shortstop record until 1902, what second baseman who also topped the NL in FA that year played beside him for the Boston Red Stockings? Your clue is that *Total Baseball* rates him as having been the best fielder in the entire league that season. Home run.

At-Bats: 15   Hits:
Potential Total Bases: 32   Total Bases:
Potential RBIs: 10   RBIs:

37. The Magic Circle

1. Who was the last 30-game winner to lose 20 in the same season? Double, and an RBI for the year it happened.

2. He was the last 20-game winner to lose 30 in the same season. Two-run homer.

3. The only rookie in the 20th century to both win and lose 20 games in his frosh season had a 20–21 record and topped the NL in complete games and innings as a yearling. RBI triple.

4. The first AL flag team to be without a 20-game winner nonetheless had seven pitchers who won 10 or more games, two of whom were Herb Pennock and Rube Bressler. Need the team and year for an RBI double.

5. The only pitcher between 1955 and 1958 to win 20 games for the Yankees, and thus an AL flag winner, bagged 21 for the first AL team to rally from a 3–1 deficit in games to win a World Series. Two bases; RBI for the year.

6. The last AL righty to win 25 games more than once, he did it three times but never for a pennant-winning club. Single.

7. The first hurler from an expansion team to net 20 wins in a season, he also copped a Cy Young Award the year he did it. RBI single.

8. The only time in this century pitchers for cellar dwellers in the same league cracked the magic circle in consecutive years happened in the AL back in 1923–24. Triple for both 20-game winners; single for one.

9. In the 1870s and early 1880s most 20-game

winners also lost 20, since teams usually had only one main pitcher and hurlers thus routinely compiled huge won-lost totals. The first pitcher to win 20 while losing less than 10 had a glittering 22–3 record and the best winning percentage in the last century by a 20-game winner. Who was he for a two-run homer?

10. The only starting pitcher to win 15 or more consecutive games in a season and fail to make the magic circle was a hurler who collected only one loss that year—and that in a season-ending appearance! RBI double.

11. He was the only southpaw ever to win 20 or more games seven years in a row. Single.

12. The first pitcher to win 20 for a last-place team that same year also became the first southpaw 20-game winner. Two-run triple.

13. The only major league franchise that had no 20-game winners between 1901–1909 had at least one almost every year after that for the next decade and a half. If you know why that's so, you must also know the team in question. Single.

14. Many Union Association hurlers won 20 games in 1884, the loop's lone year as a major league, but he was the only one to win as many as 30. Matter of fact, he won 40— and never won another game in big league livery! Why's that? Nobody really knows, but you're in standing with a two-run triple if you at least know his name.

At-Bats: 14   Hits:
Potential Total Bases: 32   Total Bases:
Potential RBIs: 14   RBIs:

38. Silver Sluggers

1. In 1988, 1,231 fewer homers were hit in the majors during the regular season than in 1987 as all 26 teams showed a decrease. Who was the only slugger among the top five home run producers in his league in 1987 who did not hit fewer homers in 1988? Tough but fair single.

2. Bill Dahlen's 15 homers in 1894 stood as a post-1893 record for shortstops until 1925 when it was broken by what soph star who hit 18 dingers and that same year became the first player ever to collect 100 or more RBIs in each of his first two seasons? Double.

3. His 22 homers in 1930 stood as a record for shortstops until the end of the decade. Double.

4. Who tagged 24 circuit clouts in 1940 after flirting for several years with breaking the season record for shortstops? Two-run single.

5. He took command of the season record for homers by a shortstop when he hammered 29 balls into the seats in 1948 and 39 a year later. RBI single.

6. Who broke the NL shortstops' season home run record of 22 that had stood for 23 years when he hit 23 four-baggers in 1953? RBI triple.

7. He became the first shortstop to crank out 40+ homers in a season when he blasted 44 in 1955. Single.

8. The only player to hit four pinch homers in

a season twice, he did it in consecutive years while playing for the Cards as a backup to Bill White. RBI triple.

9. His .170 career batting average when his home runs are deducted from his base hits is the lowest among players in the top 20 in career homers. One-run single.

10. What player twice hit 49 homers in a season and once hit 48 but never hit 50? Worth two bases.

11. Of his 78 career homers through 1990, none came in his first full season (1984) and 26— or exactly a third of his career total after eight seasons—came in 1985, giving him the all-time record for the most homers by a player who had none the previous year. RBI single.

12. His career home run percentage of 7.09 per 100 at-bats is the highest of any player active since Babe Ruth retired. Single.

13. He was a league leader in total bases no less than six times during his career but never led either league in home runs. RBI single.

14. How about a not-so-silver slugger to end on as a change of pace? In 1976 this .232-hitting third baseman led his team in homers with 11 and RBIs with 61. What's so interesting about it is that another third baseman in the same league led *his* team in homers and RBIs with almost identically lackluster stats. RBI single if you get either of the two slugging leaders and their punchless teams.

At-Bats: 14   Hits:
Potential Total Bases: 21   Total Bases:
Potential RBIs: 10   RBIs: 10

39. Their Niche Is Secure

1. Ty Cobb once led the AL in batting for nine straight years (although two of his titles are disputed). Who has the second-longest string of consecutive bat titles in AL history? Single.

2. He holds the 20th-century mark for the most consecutive years (16) at the start of a career hitting .300 or better in at least 100 games each season. Single.

3. In general a winning pitcher, on the morning of August 2, 1932, he had a losing 11–13 record for the Senators. He finished at 26–13 as he reeled off 15 straight wins, an AL record for the most consecutive victories at the end of a season. Double.

4. Karl Spooner is probably the best-known pitcher to begin his career with consecutive shutouts in his first two major league starts, but this Oriole was the last to perform the feat in September of 1966. I'll throw in that he topped AL rookie hurlers the following year with 14 wins and still award a triple.

5. What rookie set an all-time record in 1907 when he began his career by hurling 25 consecutive scoreless innings for the Phils en route to a perfect 4–0 debut with three shutouts? The following year he earned a share of another record when he was on the losing end of five 1–0 shutouts. Home run.

6. Walter Johnson set a record that's been tied but never surpassed when he threw five complete-game 1–0 shutouts in his fabulous 1912 season. What ChiSox hurler matched

Walter's record that same year—and as a rookie, no less? Nine years later, as an outfielder, he collected 75 RBIs in just 60 games, a 1.25 ribby average that also would have been a modern record if he'd maintained it for a full season. Double.

7. The first player to make 200 or more hits in a season and not hit .300 still holds the record for the most hits in a season (208) by a sub-.300 hitter. But another more monumental record he set that same year has since been broken. Double.

8. In 1970 this infielder had the fewest at-bats (399) of any player in history who took part in 150 or more games as well as the fewest total bases (89) and the lowest slugging average (.223). Two years earlier he'd set another record when he had 22 at-bats in a World Series without collecting a hit. A .217 career hitter, he's an RBI single.

9. He began his pro career at age 18 in 1939 as an outfielder and hit well but was converted to the mound because of his live arm. Finally reaching the majors in 1948 with the Cubs, he won his first four decisions and then proceeded to lose 13 straight games, a Bruin record, and was never again seen up top. A lefty all the way, he got in dutch because of his losing skein, but you're aces in my book if you know him. Grand slam homer.

10. Twelve pitchers have won 20 or more games at least seven times since 1893. Ten of the 12 are in the Hall of Fame; the other two are both eligible but have yet to be selected. Triple for both; single for one.

11. Granted, 1981 was a strike-shortened sea-

son, but that still doesn't begin to account
for why this NL team was led in homers by
a sub outfielder whose total of eight represented exactly a quarter of the club's total
production. Sac hit for the team; up to a triple if you know its leading slugger.

12. What team in 1987 gained 30 homers over its
1986 total but had a lower slugging average,
scored fewer runs, and dropped 23 games in
its won-lost record owing in part to the feeble clutch output of its third sacker, who
had 32 homers but just 69 RBIs, the fewest
ever by a player with that many dingers?
Need both the club and the player for a
single.

13. Among pitchers who had at least 175 career
decisions, his .621 winning percentage is the
highest of any southpaw who was never on
a pennant winner. Double.

At-Bats: 13   Hits:
Potential Total Bases: 29   Total Bases:
Potential RBIs: 6   RBIs:

40. Minor League Maestros

1. Called "Derby Day" because of his passion
for horse racing and in particular the Ken-
tucky Derby, he played just three games in
the majors as a 19-year-old shortstop with
the 1891 Philadelphia Athletics, but was a
renowned player-manager for years in the
high minors. With Louisville in 1903, he hit

.350 and piloted the Colonels to second place in the American Association. Switching to Columbus the following year, he won three AA pennants in the next four seasons. He also won flags for Buffalo in the International League and Wilkes-Barre in the New York State League, as well as for Louisville when he returned to the Falls City in 1916. Perhaps the most outstanding manager of his era who never got a chance to manage in the majors, and we can only wonder now why he was never given a second crack as a player either. Triple.

2. The only man to lead all minor leaguers three years in a row in homers (1952–54) he also topped all of Organized Baseball in 1946 when he creamed 48 taters. His zenith came in 1954 when he set the all-time OB record of 72 homers while playing with Roswell of the Longhorn League and also posted the all-time highest slugging average of .916. A 32-year-old first baseman at the time, he played just one more full season in OB. Two-bagger.

3. A High Point, North Carolina, native, he hit .403 as a catcher for his hometown team, then in the Piedmont League, in 1928. Twenty-one years later, back with High Point, which in the interim had combined with Thomasville and joined the North Carolina State League, he rapped .399 at age 42. One of the greatest hitting catchers ever, he hit .291 in five major league seasons, mostly with Washington, and .342 in the minors—but defensive inadequacies deprived him of the lasting recognition his bat ought to have gained him. Homer.

4. In 1929 he set an all-time OB record of 553 total bases while with the Mission Reds of the PCL. The following year, after half a season in the PCL, he was hitting .448 when he was purchased by Brooklyn, but never really got a chance to crack the Dodgers' starting outfield. A career .370 hitter in the minors, he led every top minor league of his day in batting except the AA—largely because he never spent a full season in that circuit. Still the holder of the Texas League season record for the highest batting average—.402 with San Antonio in 1923—he was rather quixotically released by the last-place Red Sox in 1925 after leading the team in hitting. Single.

5. He played for the "Miracle" Braves and fathered two major league sons, the younger of whom was the incumbent first sacker on the team that became known for the "Miracle of Coogan's Bluff" but failed to hold the job. In 1918 he led the Southern Association in batting. Five years later he embarked on a 25-year managerial career, all in the SA, that saw him bag a record nine pennants, including one in his finale in 1948 when he managed his older son, who that year set SA season records for runs scored and walks. Another who mysteriously never got a chance to pilot a big league club, his .567 winning percentage leads all men who managed more than 20 years in the minors. Triple, plus two RBIs if you also know both his sons' first names.

6. With Buffalo in 1959, this Cuban clubber led the IL in homers and RBIs to earn a shot

at the Phillies' first base post. After two so-so years with the Phils, he returned to Buffalo in 1962 and once again topped the IL in homers and RBIs. Discouraged when several more solid years in the circuit failed to gain him a second chance up top, he journeyed south of the border and spent most of his remaining OB years in the Mexican leagues. RBI double.

7. The only player since 1901 to average .400+ over a four-year span in the minors, he hit .410 for Great Falls and Salt Lake City of the Union Association between 1911 and 1914. Earlier a batting titlist in both the SA and the Pacific National League, he did well in his lone major league test and was in fact Washington's top all-around hitter in 1905 before being dropped. Generally considered to be the minors' top hitter during the dead-ball era, he'll be a tough triple for modernists.

8. After eight consecutive years with Seattle of the PCL and seven 20-win seasons, he at first refused to report when the Cubs acquired him prior to the 1943 season on the basis of his PCL-top 27 victories in 1942. Upon reluctantly joining the Bruins, he was promptly dealt to the feeble Phillies, for whom he ended his major league days in 1945 by leading the NL with 20 losses. In the minors, though, he collected 325 wins, the last ten in 1951 for Yakima of the Western International League when he was 45 years old. Known as "Kewpie," he played his first six seasons in OB as Richard Oliver, but his real handle's worth four bases.

9. Despite a belated start as a pro player—he was past 25 when he debuted in 1902—he lasted 20 years, the bulk of them with Minneapolis, where he set an AA season record in 1910 with 61 sacrifice hits. An outstanding base thief, he narrowly missed leading the AL in 1906 as a rookie with Washington, even though he spent the first quarter of the season in the minors, and was among the top five AL base stealers again in 1907, his only other year as a full-time player in the majors. That he was already past 30 was held against him, however, and not even leading the AA in runs scored four times between 1910 and 1916 and consistently ranking among that loop's top hitters could override the age handicap. A shortstop for most of his career, he was also a capable centerfielder—he played there for the White Sox for about half of the 1909 season—and could handle the job at first base too. His high point came in 1917 with Minneapolis when he hit .322 and lost the AA bat crown by a single point. Two-run homer.

10. He pitched for six teams in the PCL and was the first to win 250 games in that circuit. Born in San Francisco, he broke in with the hometown Seals in 1902 at age 20 and finished with Salt Lake City 18 years later. The Seals and the Sacramento Solons got most of his big years, but he also won 20+ twice for Los Angeles and 23 for Venice in 1913. You'll earn a three-run homer if you can spin this info into the name of this early-day 325-game winner in the minors who was last seen by fans east of the Rockies in 1907

when he toiled for Altoona of the Tri-State League.

11. In 1941 he pitched a combined total of 209 innings in four different leagues and fanned an even 300 hitters. Among them were one AL batter and 242 North East Arkansas League batters, including 25 in a nine-inning game on June 18 and 30 in an 11-inning game less than a month later. A lefty who was done in by control problems, he walked 56 men in just 79 innings in his one full major league season, 1947, split between the Browns and the Giants, and gave up 1,800 career bases on balls. But for a month in 1941 he turned the baseball world on its ear, and you'll hook a two-run homer if you know him.

12. Cut by the Cardinals after four solid but unremarkable seasons in the NL, he dropped down to Little Rock in 1916 and won a record 208 games in the SA before quitting after the 1928 season. An Arkansas native, he died in North Little Rock in 1965. Old SA followers will snag an easy RBI triple.

13. The only member of the Hockey Hall of Fame to lead a minor league in batting, he rapped .351 for Ottawa of the Border League in 1948 and also led the loop in runs and RBIs. There's naught to be said in your defense if you don't know this many-time NHL All-Star who played pro baseball for only two full seasons but major league hockey for over 20. Canadian readers will bag a snap double.

14. He had a 15–18 career OB record prior to 1920 but then joined the powerhouse Balti-

more Orioles, which won six straight IL pennants between 1920 and 1925, and finished with a .674 winning percentage, the highest of any pitcher with over 200 wins in the minors. He also pitched four years in the majors and had a brother who started the decisive seventh World Series game for Washington in 1924. Jack this one out for your sixth homer in this category.

At-Bats: 14	Hits:
Potential Total Bases: 43	Total Bases:
Potential RBIs: 14	RBIs:

41. They Spelled Relief

1. In 1989 he broke Doug Corbett's AL record for the most saves by a rookie when he notched 27. Single.
2. Mark Davis is the most recent in what's become a fairly lengthy list of relievers who've won Cy Young Awards. However, the first reliever to win an MVP Award not only never copped a Cy Young, he never even received a single vote for one. The clue that much of the reason for that is because his final season was the year the award originated knocks this down to a single, plus an RBI for the year he furthered the cause for all relievers by taking the MVP.
3. Which one of these Hall of Fame hurlers had the most career saves? Single. Bob Feller, Lefty Gomez, Bob Lemon, Red Ruffing,

Robin Roberts, Eppa Rixey, Bob Gibson, Warren Spahn, Whitey Ford.

4. This righthander worked in six of the seven games in the 1947 World Series, was the first reliever to win two games in a seven-game Series, and also saved his team's only other win. Those clues should steer you to the right team and its main stopper for an RBI single.

5. Well, then who was the first pitcher to win two games in relief in a Series of any length? It should ease your quandary if you're told it happened in the last year the Series was a 5-of-9 affair and that the hurler in question was later the first in history to oppose his brother as a starting pitcher. Two bases for the pitcher; RBI for the year.

6. The first game won in relief in a World Series was bagged by a pitcher who won five Series games all told for a team that's never won a fall championship match of any kind in which he didn't appear. Single for the pitcher; extra base for the year his team last ended fall play with a win.

7. What was the last season that a pitcher led his league in both saves and complete games? Deep thought will give you either vertigo or his name for a double, plus an RBI for the year it happened.

8. Dennis Eckersley has led the AL in saves and once almost led it in complete games; Wilbur Wood topped the AL in complete games and once almost led in saves. Who was the last pitcher to be a league leader in both departments during his career? I'll rain on your parade if you don't score a two-

bagger after being told he led the NL in one department and the AL in the other.

9. The first bullpenner to win as many as 15 games in a season in relief did it the year he surrendered the famous homer in the gloamin' to scotch his team's pennant hopes. Triple, plus an RBI for his team.

10. The first reliever to be a league leader in winning percentage, he won an amazing 23% of his team's victories in the year he broke new ground for bullpenners. RBI single.

11. In 1964 Johnny Wyatt became the first reliever to work in half his team's games. Who was the first—and to date, only—pitcher to work in two-thirds of his team's games, including post-season action? Single; RBI for the year he did it.

12. When Dan Quisenberry picked up 45 saves in 1983, whose 10-year-old record of 38 saves did he break? Single.

13. The pitching staffs of the 1906 and 1918 Boston Braves have one very significant negative stat in common. When told that they were the last two staffs in history to have this stat, you might luck into a double.

14. Which one of the following Hall of Famers was never a league leader in saves? Single. Waite Hoyt, Christy Mathewson, Walter Johnson, Cy Young, Three Finger Brown, Ed Walsh, Kid Nichols.

15. He's the only pitcher to have a season in which he led a major league in wins, winning percentage, strikeouts, ERA—and saves! Single, and take an RBI for knowing the year he did it.

At-Bats: 15   Hits:
Potential Total Bases: 22   Total Bases:
Potential RBIs: 8   RBIs:

42. Hall of Fame Hot Potatoes

1. Which of the following superstars is the only one who was not inducted into the Hall of Fame the first year he was eligible for selection despite having once gotten a vote while he was still an active player? Single. Bob Feller, Stan Musial, Willie Stargell, Warren Spahn, Joe DiMaggio, Ted Williams, Frank Robinson, Carl Yastrzemski.

2. He was the first third baseman to be voted into the HOF by regular balloting (i.e., by neither the Veterans nor the Old-Timers committees). Single.

3. He won only 53 games during his career and pitched just three full seasons in the majors, but HOF balloters thought enough of his talent and sympathized so strongly with his reasons for sitting out several years during his prime that they gave him a flock of votes between 1937 and 1955. Home run.

4. The Veterans Committee was permanently formed in 1953 and that year made its initial selection. What pitcher was their first enshrinee? RBI double.

5. He's the only player to finish among the top ten in the special Veterans Committee vote in 1936 who has never been enshrined. Moreover, he never again got more than one vote in an election, although in 1936 he was

deemed more worthy than King Kelly, Amos Rusie, and Dan Brouthers, to name just three of the many 19th-century luminaries now in the Hall. Unless you're up on your oldie stars, you're a longshot to bang a homer here.

6. In 1985 he fell only two votes short of the 297 that would have meant his enshrinement. It's the closest anyone's ever come without making it, and he's still waiting. Single.

7. Which one of the following immortals was not among the top ten finishers in 1936 when the first vote for enshrinement was taken? Single. Cy Young, Rogers Hornsby, Babe Ruth, Tris Speaker, Ty Cobb, Walter Johnson, Pete Alexander, Mickey Cochrane.

8. Even though most historians now consider the American Association to have been the equal of the National League during the decade the two circuits operated as rival major leagues, no player from the old AA has ever been enshrined. He came the closest when he got six votes from the Veterans Committee in 1936—but he's never gotten a single vote since. Rack up a homer for this slugger and base thief extraordinaire.

9. Every back-to-back pennant winner except one in the first half of this century has long since had at least one of its players make the HOF. Until the mid-1980s, the only member of this repeat champion to be enshrined was its manager. Single for the team in question, plus two RBIs for knowing both its HOF skipper and only HOF player to date.

10. Although listed on the regular HOF ballot

for years, he received a grand total of only 14 votes and just once got more than two. Yet he was enshrined in 1973 by the Veterans Committee in preference to Joe Judge and Charlie Grimm, to name two players at his position who received many more votes than he on regular ballots but have never been seriously considered for selection. Double.

11. Only one player who finished among the top ten in HOF balloting in any year between 1937 and 1960 has never been enshrined. Moreover, he rated that high twice—in 1955 and again in 1956—and got strong support in virtually every year prior to 1960. He's a catcher, and you'll snag a three-bagger if you nail him.

12. Only four catchers who were active a minimum of ten seasons retired with .300+ career batting averages. Three are in the HOF; the fourth almost certainly never will be despite hitting a career .308, perhaps because he was the Phils' regular backstopper in the period when they had some of the worst pitching staffs ever assembled. Take a homer for this tough but utterly fair question that truly belongs here.

13. The last pitcher to win 30 games more than once and not make the HOF did it both before and after the mound was moved to its present distance from the plate. And he also once won 29 games. Two-run homer.

14. The 1927 Yankees, perhaps the strongest team ever, had five players make the HOF. What rival AL club has seven players from its 1927 cast now in the HOF? Your clues,

should you really need them, are that this team also had seven Famers in 1928 to make it the only AL club in history to have that many Famers in back-to-back seasons, and that despite all that super talent it came away empty-handed as the Yankees once again romped to the flag. Single for the club; home run if you can name all seven of its HOF inductees who could do no better in 1927 than a second-place finish, 19 games back of the Yankees.

15. Among the many who have received HOF votes are such undistinguished players as Morrie Martin, Bob Kuzava, Fred Leach, Cy Perkins, and Dode Paskert. What player who was active 18 seasons, made 2,502 hits, ranks 24th in career runs, among the top 50 in both career doubles and triples, hit .320 or better at various times in three different leagues—the National, the Players, and the American—and rapped more career homers than such contemporary sluggers as Dan Brouthers and Hugh Duffy has not received a single vote from any HOF committee, ever? Do yourself proud and end with a two-run homer.

At-Bats: 15   Hits:
Potential Total Bases 40   Total Bases:
Potential RBIs: 14   RBIs:

OCTOBER

Twin Spoilers

In Game 2 of the 1988 World Series, Orel Hershiser of the Dodgers pitched a masterful three-hit 6–0 shutout against the A's. All three hits that Hershiser surrendered were singles made by the same man. His super performance, all that stood between Hershiser and the second World Series no-hitter in history, had been almost exactly paralleled 65 years earlier. On October 13, 1923, in the last home game the Yankees ever played in the Polo Grounds, their hurler that day was deprived of immortality and a shutout when a certain Giants slugger collected all three of his team's hits—a single, double, and triple! Bag a one-base hit by naming the lone A's hitter able to solve Hershiser in his 6–0 shutout. Take two more bases if you know the Yankees righthander whose three-hitter topped the Giants 8–1 in Game 6 of the 1923 Series. And pick up two RBIs for the Giants swatter who provided all of his team's punch in that contest.

43. Fall Favorites

1. Who was the only man to win three games in his first World Series appearance and play another position in his one other taste of fall competition? RBI single.
2. He was the last pitcher to win three games

in either a World Series or a League Championship Series. Single, plus an extra base for the year he did it.

3. This Yankees catcher was on six World Series teams but got into only one Series contest. At that he was luckier than a Yankees backstopper from an earlier era who set a record by being on five World Series teams without ever making a single fall appearance. Name both for a homer; single if you know just one of them.

4. The first team to use all its eligible players in a World Series did it in a five-game classic in which it won only Game 2, 1–0, after losing the Series opener by an identical score. The club had 25 eligible players, Jack Banta was its only pitcher to appear in more than one game, and Luis Olmo and Gene Hermanski were its two most productive outfielders offensively. Now, name that team for a single; RBI for the year.

5. In 1987 both the Cardinals and the Twins used all their eligible players in the World Series. The only other time both Series contestants did that was in a seven-game Series that saw Bob Oldis, Joe Christopher, and Fred Green participate for the winners and Eli Grba, Joe DeMaestri, and Dale Long for the losers. Need both teams and the year it happened for a double.

6. When the Indians were swept in four straight in 1954, a future Hall of Famer rode the bench for the entire World Series. What team that was swept in an earlier WS had *two* future Famers ride the wood the entire

way? Gotta have the team and both players for an RBI triple.

7. Which one of the following 19th-century stars was never on a 20th-century World Series roster? Single. Bobby Lowe, Buck Freeman, Bill Dahlen, George Davis, Lave Cross, Kip Selbach, Duke Farrell, Brickyard Kennedy.

8. What were the only two years that teams were allowed to exceed 25-man rosters in the WS and what was the reason for the exemption? Clues: in the first year the Series losers carried 31 men, including Cy Block, Walter Signer, and Len Rice, and in the second year the winners carried 30, including Walt Sessi, Bill Endicott, and Jeff Cross. Two bases for the years; RBI for the explanation.

9. The first seven-game World Series in which no pitcher on either team bagged more than one victory was the only Series in which a team batted .000 against a rival pitcher for an entire game. With a clue like that, who can miss this single?

10. The first player to make 12 hits in a WS did it for a losing team in a match that went eight games owing to a tie. Two; sac hit if you know just the year and his team.

11. In 1964 Bobby Richardson of the Yankees became the first player to garner 13 hits in a WS. He was not the leading batter that fall, however. That honor went to what opposition player and present-day media guy who rapped .478 for the seven-game match? RBI single.

12. The first man to hit .500 while playing every

game of a WS that went more than five games did it for a team that was beaten three times by Red Faber. Also the first player to hit safely in every game of a Series that went longer than five games, he was twice an NL homer king. Double, and an RBI for the year.

13. The first player to hit home runs in two consecutive World Series was the second National Leaguer to play against his brother in a WS. Double.

14. He made three plate appearances as a pinch hitter in World Series play, all of them in 1924, and a set a WS record for the most trips to the plate without being credited with an at-bat when Giant hurlers walked him on all three occasions. Three-run homer.

15. The only World Series in which catchers led both the winning team and the losing team in batting went just four games and saw both backstoppers top the .500 mark. Knowing that both were MVPs during their careers should enable you to get them and the year as well for a double.

At-Bats: 15   Hits:
Potential Total Bases: 30   Total Bases:
Potential RBIs: 9   RBIs:

44. Their Niche Is Secure

1. He rang everyone's chimes in Ontario when he kicked off the 1988 season by becoming

the first player to clout three home runs in an Opening Day game. Single.

2. Traded to the Reds a few weeks earlier, this 34-year-old bammer proved he wasn't washed up, as many Cinci critics of the deal had contended, when he became the only player in NL history to collect six hits and three home runs in the same game. Happened on July 6, 1949, and you can walk to a three-bagger if you happened to catch this guy's coup.

3. Clint Courtney was the first catcher to wear glasses in an AL game. Okay, probably most of you knew that, but I'll stake a two-run homer it'll be news to just about everybody who the first backstopper was to do the same in an NL game.

4. The Philadelphia A's had many Hall of Famers during their 54-year history. He'll probably never make the Hall, but he will always hold the Philadelphia A's career record for runs scored and also the team record for the most home runs by a rookie. Never on a flag winner, he's worth an RBI double.

5. The holder of the Brooklyn Dodgers' rookie season home run record was a first sacker, but his name wasn't Hodges or Camilli. RBI triple.

6. Mark McGwire set not only a rookie record but also the Oakland A's season record for most homers when he slammed 49 four-baggers as a frosh. What's the only other team in existence between 1903 and 1990 that has its season home run record held by a rookie? Two for the team; RBI for the yearling star.

7. The Yankees have had a switch hitter and

two lefty hitters crack 50 or more homers in a season. What's the only team that's had both a lefthanded and righthanded hitter top the 50 barrier? Single; RBI for the two clubbers.

8. Frankly, his main claim to fame may just be that he was the first man in major league history to win 200 games without ever scoring a run. Single.

9. It seems like it's been an unwelcome part of the game for years now, but actually it was only a little over a decade ago that the first player in major league history was suspended for a drug-related offense. Your clues are that he was busted outside the USA on September 9, 1980, and reinstated 13 days later. Single.

10. Prior to Pete Rose's rookie year, who held the Reds' record for the most years of active service as a player (pitchers excepted)? Rough homer even after you're made privy to the fact that his younger brother is the only player in big league history to hit .370 or better in his lone year as a regular.

11. Bob Feller set a post-1893 record when he K'd 18 Tigers in a game in 1938, but his feat came in a losing cause. What hurler also lost the game—4-3 to the Mets—in which he broke Feller's record? RBI single.

12. Just once since 1893 has a pitcher lost 20 games for a pennant winner. We met him in another book of mine, but I've yet to meet anyone who can rattle off the names of the only other two hurlers in major league history to drop 20 or more games for a first-place team. Your clues are each lost 21, nei-

ther is in the Hall of Fame, one was one of
the greatest hitting pitchers ever, and the
other had 181 wins before his 25th birthday.
Grand slam for both; two-run double for
either.

13. The only man to play 20 seasons in a Cleveland uniform was never on a flag winner but
served as the pitching coach for the last
Tribe team to win a World Championship.
Two-bagger.

At-Bats: 13   Hits:
Potential Total Bases: 29   Total Bases:
Potential RBIs: 12   RBIs:

45. Great Glovemen

1 1. He's the only member of the top ten list for
the best career fielding average by a second
baseman who was active in the majors prior
to 1950. Double.

2. He's the only member of the top ten list for
the best career fielding average by an outfielder who was active in the majors prior to
1950. RBI double.

3. He's the only member of the top ten list for
the best career fielding average by a catcher
who was active in the majors prior to 1950.
Even after slipping you the clue that he was
once a teammate of the lone second baseman
with the same credentials, I'll still award a
double.

4. He alone among the members of the top ten

list for the best career fielding average by a first baseman was active prior to 1950—and what's more, he was around before 1940. Three bases.

5. The only infielder, outfielder, or catcher on this wave length we're pursuing at the moment who's in the Hall of Fame was also around before 1940. Name both him and the position at which he excelled for a single.

6. He never won a Gold Glove, but in 1971 he became the first Met to be a league leader in fielding average. Being told that he narrowly beat out Dennis Menke that year will help experts but probably just send others off the high board. Two-run double.

7. Johnny Bench and he are the only NL catchers to win four or more Gold Gloves. Easy double for historians; modernists will likely fan here.

8. He led the A's with 120 RBIs the year after he established a new major league mark (since broken) for the top fielding average by a third baseman. Clues are right for the regal to score three bases here.

9. The last black catcher to win a Gold Glove, he copped two during his illustrious career. Single.

10. He led all NL shortstops in double plays in 1950 despite committing 51 errors. Twenty-nine years later his son set a new major league record for shortstops (since broken) when he helped turn 144 twin-kills. Just murmur the family name for a single.

11. Hornsby, Frisch, and Gehringer were the top offensive second basemen during this man's heyday (1926–36), but none of them

could carry his glove. He holds the AL career record for the most assists per game, plus the 20th-century career record for the most total chances per game, and in 1933 fielded .991, a figure that stood until 1948 as the best ever by a second sacker. Solo homer.

12. In 1919, when the Red Sox led the AL with a .975 FA, what shortstop of theirs set a new major league fielding record mark of .976? A year later he again topped the Sox team fielding average, making him the only shortstop in history to perform this feat in successive seasons while playing for a club that won back-to-back league fielding honors. Snatch three bases for this forgotten glove great.

At-Bats: 12   Hits:
Potential Total Bases: 26   Total Bases:
Potential RBIs: 4   RBIs:

46. Fall Favorites

1. In 1975, despite being the first player to hit safely in every game of a seven-game World Series, he hit below .300—in fact, just .267. Three years later his brother, a career .161 hitter, rapped .438 and led all Series batters. Need both for an RBI double; sac hit for just knowing the family name.

2. The only team to win a World Series without a single player who hit as high as .275 was led by _____'s .263 average and game-

winning homer in the bottom of the ninth inning of the opener. Your clue is his team hit just .226 but won in five games because its hurlers held the opposition to a .210 average and only 14 runs. Two-bagger if you get both him and his team.

3. The only member of an AL team that was swept to lead all hitters in that year's World Series, he cracked .500 and garnered eight hits in a losing cause that might have gone the other way if he'd a ninth that seemed a triple at the very least when it left his bat in the opening game. Two-run single.

4. What Cubs third baseman was the first member of an NL team that was swept to lead all Series hitters in both hits and batting average? Two-bagger, and a bonus two RBIs for the NL shortstop who hit .429 to lead all hitters in a later Series while playing for a team that was swept.

5. The last WS to be concluded without a single home run being hit was in 1918. What was the first WS that featured 10 or more homers? Clue: among those who contributed to the dinger total were Aaron Ward and Pancho Snyder. Two bases.

6. The most home runs in a WS is 17; it's been done twice. On both occasions the same two franchises participated, but one did it while representing two different cities. Sandy Amoros hit one of the winning team's homers on the first occasion, and Chris Chambliss homered once for the winners on the second occasion. Name both teams and the years in question for a double.

7. In the 1926 WS, Babe Ruth's four homers

matched the Cardinals' total circuit-clout output as four different Birds connected. Among them were a pitcher who hit just three others in his 19-year career and a shortstop who played 12 more years in the majors without ever homering again. Take four bases for this pair of unlikely home run contributors; single for one.

8. The first team to have two pitchers homer in a WS lost the clash even though each of the hurlers won the game he connected in. Two-run homer for both chuckers and their team and year; double if you know just one man.

9. Mike Moore of the A's broke a ten-year hit-less drought by AL pitchers in WS action when he tripled in Game 4 of the 1989 session. The last AL pitcher to make two hits in a Series also won two games that year—but his team still lost in seven. Who was he? Triple.

10. The last AL pitcher to homer in a WS game connected off Andy Messersmith and was also the last AL pitcher to hit .500 in a Series. Two-bagger.

11. Tom Zachary compiled a perfect 3–0 record as a starting pitcher in WS play with two different teams, the Senators and Yankees. Who did even better, posting a 5–0 mark not only with two different teams in two different leagues? Double, plus an RBI for the hurler's two teams.

12. Which one of the following 200-game winners never lost a World Series game? Single. Vic Willis, Lou Burdette, Hal Newhouser,

Carl Mays, Rube Marquard, Jerry Koosman, Vida Blue, Jim Palmer.

13. Babe Ruth's record of 11 walks, set in the 1926 WS, was tied by what slugging star of the first WS won by the last team to bag three consecutive World Championships? Single.

14. The only player to hit two homers in a game twice in the same WS did it for a losing team but each time on behalf of the same starting pitcher. Triple, plus an RBI for the pitcher he so valiantly supported.

15. Mickey Mantle hit a record 18 homers in 12 World Series and 65 games. What Hall of Famer appeared in eight WS and had 197 at-bats without ever homering in fall play? Clue: he's tied with Yogi Berra for the most career Series doubles. Two-bagger.

At-Bats: 15   Hits:
Potential Total Bases: 34   Total Bases:
Potential RBIs: 10   RBIs:

47. Team Teasers

1. If asked what World Championship team was shut out the most times (16) in a 154-game season, you'll of course shout the Hit-less Wonders. But do you know what later flag winner, playing a 162-game schedule, was blanked a record 17 times and then thrice more in the World Series? Team and year for a single.

2. The year before it won its first flag, this team fanned a record 1,203 times with such players as Jerry Buchek, who collected 53 whiffs in just 192 at-bats. I'll toss in that the club finished only one game out of the cellar even though its pitchers gave up just 499 runs, the fewest ever by a second-division team playing a 162-game schedule, and still credit an RBI single.

3. After learning that its mound leader was Weldon Wyckoff with 10 wins and that Jimmy Walsh led with 22 steals, can you name the team that used an all-time record 56 players in the course of the season? Single; extra base for the year.

4. What team drew an all-time record 835 walks, spearheaded by a man who that year led the AL in walks for the record sixth consecutive season he was on active playing status? Single, plus an RBI for its chief walk gatherer.

5. On May 23, 1901, two bad teams, both of whom were destined to finish deep in the second division that year, met up in a game that ought to have been a sportswriter's nightmare. Instead it became a classic when the home team, after trailing 13–5 with two out in the ninth, came on to win 14–13 in the greatest two-out ninth-inning comeback in history. I'll tell you the two clubs were managed by Jimmy Manning and Jimmy McAleer, and the game was played west of the Allegheny; now tell me both the winning and losing teams for a triple.

6. The longest AL game and also the longest AL night game occurred on May 8, 1984, and

was suspended by curfew and finished the next day. If told the home team won 7–6 in 25 innings, no other American League cities are closer than the two whose teams were involved in this game, and the game was played in the AL's oldest park at the time, name both participants for a deuce.

7. The longest game played entirely on one day to a decision was on September 11, 1974, and was also the NL's longest night game. Can you name the two clubs that participated in it once you know that both were managed by Hall of Famers? Single, plus an RBI for naming the winning team.

8. Despite not coming into existence until 1903, the Yankees have won by far the most games of any AL franchise. Take two if you know what AL club has won the second-most games since 1901.

9. What team lost 100 or more games for a record five straight seasons? Single for the team; extra base for the five-year span.

10. This team finished a 20th-century record 66½ games behind the pennant winner in its league one year. Once you know the club won 49 games and lost 102, math alone should tell you what season this happened and who finished 66½ games ahead of our lads that season. Need both clubs for a double.

11. Only once has a team won the pennant despite being in last place on July 4, albeit only 15 games back. The club's an easy single, but you can nail a tough RBI if you know its startling margin of victory at the season's close.

12. When the Cubs failed to win a pennant in 1988 for the 43rd straight year, whose all-time record for being pennantless did they break? Single.

13. The only mound staff in this century to give up less than 300 walks (295) was led by a lefty whose 20 wins sparked the team to the pennant. A tough question grows easy when I note that he was the club's sole 20-game winner in a four-year span that saw it cop four flags. Need the team, year, and lefty for two.

14. What franchise holds the all-time record for the largest crowd for a twin bill, the largest crowd for a night game and the largest crowd for an All-Star Game—plus its league's marks for the largest crowd for a day game, World Series game, and Opening Day game? Single.

At-Bats: 14   Hits:
Potential Total Bases: 22   Total Bases:
Potential RBIs: 4   RBIs:

48. Their Last Hurrah

1. His last major league start nearly resulted in the first World Series no-hitter, but he was robbed of both immortality and the game on a two-out, two-run double in the bottom of the ninth inning. You're a sharp cookie if you can garner a double by naming both him

and his foiler, whose pinch blow was ironically his last major league hit.

2. He collected 218 hits and ripped .382 in his coda season. Obviously he wasn't dumped because he'd lost it talent-wise. Enough clues there to single.

3. His 34 homers and 94 RBIs are both tops among players in their final seasons. But, rats, his .236 batting average is a career low for first basemen with over 3,000 at-bats. Single.

4. He's the lone member of the 3,000-hit club to appear in more than 100 games in the field in his final bow. RBI single.

5. He's the lone Hall of Famer who made it solely on the basis of his playing credentials but never retired as an active player. Single.

6. He fell a mere 13 hits short of being the second outfielder in ten years to make his 3,000th hit in a Cleveland uniform when he quit after hitting .293 for the Tribe in 1934. Double, plus an extra base for the 3,000-hit gardener.

7. He became the first righthanded pitcher in nearly 40 years to win 300 games when he beat the Kansas City A's in his last major league start. Single.

8. He's the only slugger to hit both his 500th homer and more than 20 four-baggers in his last hurrah. Single.

9. He hit .373 and knocked home 124 runs before an off-season stroke brought an abrupt and premature end to his glittering career. RBI double.

10. His 234 total bases are the most of any player in his final campaign who was neither

barred from the game nor forced to quit for health reasons. You're in tip-top shape if you know the team with which he began his finale, which saw him hit .308 and lead his circuit in doubles. Homer.

11. The only non-DH in this century to collect over 90 RBIs in his last season, he was also the first and to date only BoSox hurler to win 30 games in a season since the schedule was increased to at least 154 games. RBI single.

12. He's the only player ever to smack three homers in a game in his final season. Single.

13. Only once in history has a pitcher stood either to win or lose a pennant in his final major league start. It should help plenty to know that he toiled for a team that was heavily favored that day to win its second flag in three years but instead his opponents blew him out and won their first bunting in 28 years. Triple.

14. He was cut by the White Sox after the 1925 season and his shortstop post given to Bill Hunnefield even though he scored 105 runs, the most in this century by a player in his final season who didn't leave the game under a cloud. Three-run homer to break the string, but no alibis if you miss it.

15. He's the only player to rank first in career games played at his position and perform in over 100 games at that position in his finale. RBI single.

At-Bats: 15   Hits:
Potential Total Bases: 26 Total Bases:
Potential RBIs: 7   RBIs:

49. Fall Favorites

1. Playing in his first World Series game, he smacked a record five hits in the Series opener and got two more the next day to tie another record for the most hits in two consecutive games. But he made just four more hits in the remaining five games as his team fell in seven to Whitey's only World Championship squad. Single.

2. Playing in a WS that lasted just six games, he set a record for a Series of any length when he fanned 12 times for the team that lost to the last of the original 16 franchises to win its first WS. Enough there to score both the player and year for a single.

3. This one's a pip, but here goes. The winning pitcher of the game in which Babe Ruth's reputed "Called Shot" homer occurred also became that same day the first player to fan five times in a WS contest. Name him for three.

4. One big reason the Dodgers won their first World Championship in 1955 was the enormous assist Brooklyn pitchers were given by what Yankees outfielder who grounded into a record five double plays and had just one hit in 16 at-bats? RBI double.

5. The last WS in which the winning pitcher in each contest hurled a complete game was won in seven games by a team that lost the first two contests in the most recently built stadium that has since been razed. RBI single.

6. He and Bill Carrigan are the only two man-

agers to pilot more than one WS-winning club without ever being at the helm of a Series loser. Double.

7. Several managers headed teams that were swept in their lone taste of Series action as helmsmen. Who's the only one who was also on a sweep victim as a player? Double, plus an RBI for the two years in question.

8. Which one of the following Hall of Fame pitchers never won a Series game? Single. Bob Lemon, Walter Johnson, Joe McGinnity, Eddie Plank, Ed Walsh, Dazzy Vance, Dizzy Dean, Burleigh Grimes, Cy Young.

9. The last WS that ended in a tie showcased the Bridegrooms and the Cyclones. Obviously we're not talking about a modern WS and, perhaps less obviously, both teams are better known to most readers by other nicknames. Now, for a triple, nail the year it happened and the two clubs, neither of which was the best in the majors that year (probably your biggest clue of all right there). Plus two RBIs for the team that won the flag in the league that had most of the top talent that season.

10. The 1938 Yankees used four pitchers and just 14 players in drubbing the Cubs. But another club was even more parsimonious, using a record-low two pitchers and only 12 players to beat the Cubs in an earlier Series that went five games. Among the members of the team who saw no action were Claude Derrick, Rube Oldring, and a Hall of Fame pitcher. Team and year for a deuce; RBI for the HOF hurler who sat and watched.

11. The only pitcher to win two complete games

for the last team to win back-to-back World Championships didn't appear in a team's second fall clash but was still highly instrumental in its getting to the Series, albeit in a way he'd rather forget. Who was he and what'd he do to help the cause? Single.

12. The first year two Rookies of the Year opposed each other in a WS was also the season that a rookie who did not win the frosh award led the NL in ERA and another rookie also-ran led the AL in triples. The year, both rookie winners, and both rookie runners-up will bring an RBI triple; single for less.

13. The Rookie of the Year Award was first given officially in 1947, the MVP Award began back in 1931, and the Cy Young in 1956. What was the first WS in which *neither* participant had any of its league's three major award winners? May help to know that Bob Parsons was the Rookie of the Year runner-up in the AL that year and Jerry Johnson finished sixth in Cy Young balloting in the NL. Double.

14. Finish with a very generous RBI single by zeroing right in on the first World Series to feature both Cy Young winners and both MVPs. What makes it so generous is the clue that two men took all four awards that year.

At-Bats: 14	Hits:
Potential Total Bases: 25	Total Bases:
Potential RBIs: 7	RBIs:

ANSWERS

April

Bottomley's Dozen: Wilbert Robinson and Branch Rickey (not Rogers Hornsby!)

1. Their Niche is Secure

1. Wade Boggs
2. Nolan Ryan, 1972
3. Max Bishop
4. Luke Appling
5. Herb Score
6. Bob Horner
7. Nap Lajoie
8. Billy Herman
9. Ted Williams
10. Roberto Clemente; .328, 1960s
11. Ted Simmons
12. Red Ruffing
13. Pete Alexander, 1915–17
14. Pie Traynor
15. Rabbit Maranville

2. Pitching Posers

1. Don Sutton
2. Jim McCormick, Scotland
3. Bill James, 1914
4. Gaylord Perry
5. Ed Walsh, 1908
6. Jack Chesbro, 1904
7. Bob Feller in 1946
8. Catfish Hunter, 1975
9. Rick Langford in 1980
10. Fernando Valenzuela
11. Jim Clancy, Blue Jays
12. Billy Hoeft
13. Pink Hawley and Frank Killen
14. Luis Tiant, 1969
15. Pirates, Murray Dickson

3. Dynamite Duos

1. Babe Ruth and Lou Gehrig.
2. Hack Wilson and Kiki Cuyler
3. Hack Wilson and Rogers Hornsby
4. Roger Maris and Mickey Mantle, 1961
5. Joe DiMaggio and Lou Gehrig in 1937
6. Willie Mays and Willie McCovey; Johnny Mize and Willard Marshall
7. Babe Ruth and Lou Gehrig, 1927
8. Elmer Flick and Ed Delahanty, 1900
9. Harry Davis and Lave Cross, 1905 Athletics
10. George Foster and Joe Morgan in 1976
11. Philadelphia; Don Hurst and Chuck Klein of the Phils, Jimmie Foxx and Al Simmons of the A's
12. 1928 Yankees; Babe Ruth, Lou Gehrig, and Bob Meusel
13. 1915 Tigers; Bobby Veach, Sam Crawford, and Ty Cobb
14. 1952 Indians; Larry Doby and Luke Easter in homers, Al Rosen and Larry Doby in RBIs, Bob Lemon, Mike Garcia, and Early Wynn all won 20.
15. Ty Cobb and Sam Crawford, 1908–11

4. All in the Family

1. Felipe and Matty Alou, 1966
2. Ken Griffey Sr. and Ken Jr.
3. Mort and Walker Cooper, 1944 Cardinals
4. Joe and Luke Sewell; Yankees and Senators
5. The Clarksons
6. Hank Aaron
7. Lee and Jesse Tannehill
8. Lou and Dino Chiozza, 1935 Phils
9. John, Tom, and Jim Paciorek
10. Dane and Garth Iorg
11. Dennis Rasmussen and Bill Brubaker
12. Bobby and Barry Bonds
13. Jim and John O'Rourke
14. Mark and Paul Christman

5. Batting Title Bafflers

1. The first two bat titlists from last-place teams in their respective leagues
2. Harvey Kuenn and Al Kaline in 1959
3. Roberto Clemente
4. Frank Robinson
5. Carl Furillo, 1953
6. Buddy Myer
7. Hal McRae
8. Ferris Fain, 1952
9. George Sisler and George Stone
10. Luke Appling
11. Ernie Lombardi, 1942
12. Zach Wheat
13. Rogers Hornsby, 1922
14. Jimmie Foxx, 1938

6. The Magic Circle

1. Warren Spahn
2. Charlie Buffington
3. Pud Galvin
4. Steve Carlton
5. Early Wynn
6. Robin Roberts
7. 1931; Heine Meinie, Bill Hallahan, and Jumbo Elliott
8. BoBo Newsom; 1934 Browns; 1941 Tigers, 1945 A's
9. Early Wynn
10. Roger Craig; 1962–63
11. Bob Lemon (7), Bob Feller (6), Early Wynn (5), Hal Newhouser (4), Mike Garcia (2)
12. Frank Lary, Bucky Harris
13. Randy Jones
14. Bob Gibson

7. Home Run Leaders

1. Cy Williams, Phils and Cubs; Johnny Mize, Cards and Giants; Dave Kingman, Cubs and Mets
2. Reggie Jackson; A's, Yankees, and Angels
3. Sam Crawford
4. 1981 strike season; Eddie Murray, Dwight Evans, Bobby Grich, and Tony Armas
5. Ralph Kiner
6. Babe Ruth, Lou Gehrig, Joe DiMaggio, and Bob Meusel
7. Gorman Thomas
8. Mike Schmidt
9. Harry Davis, 1904–07
10. Johnny Bench, 1970, 1972
11. Bill Nicholson
12. George Foster, 1977–78
13. Tim Jordan
14. Hank Greenberg, 1935 when he tied Jimmie Foxx
15. Johnny Mize, Ted Williams, Joe DiMaggio, and Hank Greenberg

MAY

The Short-Lived Record: Jim Deshaies, 1986, Dodgers; Mickey Welch; Joe Cowley

8. No-Hitter Nuggets

1. Bob Feller
2. Allie Reynolds
3. Howard Ehmke
4. Lon Warneke, the "Arkansas Hummingbird"
5. Johnny Vander Meer
6. Sandy Koufax
7. Addie Joss
8. Bumpus Jones
9. Bill Hawke
10. Earl Moore
11. Bo Belinsky
12. Pud Galvin, Buffalo
13. 1913
14. Pete Alexander
15. 84; Lee Richmond and Monte Ward threw the only previous ones in 1880, though Harvey Haddix *lost* a PG in 1959

9. Silver Sluggers

1. Rogers Hornsby, 1922
2. Rogers Hornsby and Bill Terry
3. Jimmie Foxx, 1936
4. Pat Seerey
5. Roger Maris
6. Ted Williams in 1953
7. Eddie Sanicki
8. Mickey Mantle, 1961
9. Joe Rudi
10. Rogers Hornsby; Cardinals, Braves, and Cubs; Mel Ott of the Giants; Hack Wilson of the Cubs
11. Dave Parker and Don Mattingly, 1985–86
12. Frank Robinson
13. Eddie Mathews, 1953
14. Don Mincher

10. Terrific Tandems

1. Jack Chesbro and Jack Powell of the 1904 Yankees
2. 1944 Tigers; Hal Newhouser and Dizzy Trout
3. 1924 Dodgers; Dazzy Vance and Burleigh Grimes
4. Mark Baldwin and Silver King; Players League; Charlie Comiskey
5. Sandy Koufax and Don Drysdale of the 1965 Dodgers
6. Joe McGinnity and Christy Mathewson of the 1904 Giants
7. Jim Bagby and Stan Coveleski
8. Orioles; 1960, 1970, and 1980; Chuck Estrada (18) and Milt Pappas (15) in 1960
9. Reds; Dolph Luque and Pete Donohue
10. Hoss Radbourn and Charlie Sweeney; 1884 Providence Grays
11. 1974 Angels; Nolan Ryan and Frank Tanana
12. 1899 Cleveland Spiders; Jim Hughey and Charlie Knepper
13. Red Sox; Boo Ferriss and Tex Hughson in 1946; Mel Parnell and Ellis Kinder in 1949
14. 1963; Whitey Ford and Jim Bouton

11. Managerial Musings

1. Dodgers, Harry Lumley in 1909
2. Joe McCarthy, 1931–46, Yankees
3. Pirates, Fred Clarke
4. Dick Williams, John McNamara, and Jimmy Dykes
5. Bill McKechnie; Pirates, Cards, and Reds
6. 1977 Rangers; Frank Lucchesi, Eddie Stanky, Connie Ryan, and Billy Hunter
7. Fred Mitchell of the 1918 Cubs
8. Wilbert Robinson (Hugh Jennings never played a full season under McGraw)
9. Mickey Cochrane
10. Clark Griffith, 1901 White Sox
11. Bucky Harris
12. Tris Speaker, 1920
13. Donie Bush (Joe Tinker won an FL flag with the 1915 Chicago Whales)
14. Bill McKechnie, 1925 Pirates

12. Their Niche Is Secure

1. Lamarr Hoyt, 1985
2. Honus Wagner
3. Nope, not Bench—Yogi Berra
4. Ted Williams
5. Mickey Cochrane
6. Manny Sanguillen
7. Tommy Byrne in 1949
8. Rube Waddell, 1903–05
9. Mudcat Grant, 1965
10. Gene Tenace
11. Roger Connor, home runs
12. Honus Wagner, Luke Appling and Arky Vaughan
13. Walter Johnson
14. Ben Cantwell, 1935 Braves
15. Bob Caruthers and Guy Hecker, 1886

13. Great Glovemen

1. Bobby Shantz
2. Vic Power
3. Clete and Ken Boyer
4. Frank Malzone, Brooks Robinson
5. Mickey Stanley
6. Rick Manning in 1976
7. Mike Squires, 1981
8. Dale Murphy
9. Chicago; Luis Aparicio, Nellie Fox, and Ernie Banks; Bill Mazeroski
10. Frank Lary
11. Jimmy Piersall
12. Bob Boone; Johnny Bench and Jim Sundberg

14. Team Teasers

1. Royals, 1977
2. Red Sox, 1906
3. 1899 Cleveland Spiders
4. New York Giants
5. White Sox, Bill Melton
6. Browns, 1922
7. Cleveland
8. White Sox and Senators
9. 1969–71 Orioles
10. Cardinals, 1942–44
11. Cubs, 1906–09
12. Mets in 1962
13. 1965 Yankees, managed by Johnny Keane
14. 1951 Giants
15. 1948 Indians

JUNE

The Enigmatic Walk Leaders: Roy Cullenbine and Hank Greenberg, teammates on the 1938 and 1946 Tigers

15. Pitching Posers

1. Wilbur Wood, 1971–75
2. Chief Bender
3. Ike Delock
4. Warren Spahn
5. Buddy Daley
6. Dick Bosman
7. Jim Kaat
8. Larry Dierker
9. Paul Splittorff
10. Charlie Root
11. Wilbur Cooper
12. Cy Young
13. Urban Shocker
14. Barney Pelty
15. Urban Shocker once again

16. Their Niche Is Secure

1. Al Simmons
2. Roy Campanella
3. Gabby Hartnett
4. Vern Stephens
5. Dale Mitchell; fanned to end Don Larsen's perfect game
6. Al Simmons
7. Walt Dropo
8. Hugh Jennings
9. Arky Vaughan, 1935
10. Fred Dunlap; hit .412 to lead the Union Association in 1884, its lone year as a major league
11. Bill Hutchinson, 1892
12. Rocky Colavito
13. Luis Tiant in 1968
14. Home Run Baker
15. Buck Weaver

17. Men in Blue

1. Bill Klem
2. Bill Dinneen
3. Honest John Gaffney
4. Bill Haller in 1972
5. Bill McKinley
6. Art Williams
7. Billy McLean
8. The umpires went on strike to gain salary increases and recognition of the Major League Umpires Association
9. George Hildebrand
10. Jake Beckley
11. Cal Hubbard
12. George Moriarty
13. Jocko Conlon
14. Billy Evans
15. Tom Connolly

18. Wondrous Wildmen

1. Steve Carlton
2. Bump Hadley
3. Amos Rusie
4. Mark Baldwin
5. Bob Feller
6. Elmer Myers
7. BoBo Newsom
8. Joe Coleman, Jr.
9. Sam Jones
10. Earl Moore
11. Jeff Tesreau
12. "El Goofo"— Lefty Gomez
13. Early Wynn
14. Henry and Christy Mathewson

19. Silver Sluggers

1. Dave Kingman, Jose Cruz
2. Roy Campanella, 1953
3. Gabby Hartnett in 1930
4. Yogi Berra
5. Jimmy Dykes, Nap Lajoie
6. Tony Lazzeri
7. Nate Colbert
8. John Mayberry, Royals
9. Ted Williams, 1957
10. Gavvy Cravath, 1915
11. Cards, Jack Clark
12. George Sisler; George Kelly; Cap Anson
13. Eddie Mathews, Juan Marichal
14. Babe Ruth (714), Jimmie Foxx (534), Ted Williams (521), Mel Ott (511), Lou Gehrig (493), Stan Musial (429 through 1960), Ralph Kiner (369), Duke Snider (368 through 1960), Joe DiMaggio (361), Johnny Mize (358)

20. Thieves Like Us

1. 1948, Bob Dillinger and Richie Ashburn
2. Amos Otis
3. Frank Chance
4. Max Carey
5. Ray Schalk
6. Dave Collins, 1980
7. Freddie Patek, 1977
8. Pepper Martin
9. George Case
10. Eddie Collins
11. Josh Devore
12. 1934 Tigers; Jo-Jo White, Pete Fox, and Gee Walker
13. Amos Otis
14. Vince Coleman, 1989
15. Lou Gehrig, Ted Williams (fewest)

21. Be It Ever So Humble

1. Cubs
2. Indians
3. Pirates, Forbes Field
4. Yankees
5. Astros, 1965
6. Angels, Wrigley Field
7. Twins, Metrodome
8. Jarry Park, the Expos' first home
9. Jack Murphy Stadium, Padres
10. 1974, Yankees and Mets shared Shea
11. Fenway's Green Monster
12. Blue Jays; Exhibition Stadium; Toronto Argonauts
13. Boston Braves: 1915; South End Grounds
14. Milwaukee County Stadium

JULY

The Towering Twosome: Ty Cobb and Nap Lajoie, 1910

22. Batting Title Bafflers

1. Snuffy Stirnweiss in 1945
2. Paul Waner, who would have won in 1926–27
3. Taffy Wright in 1938, Jimmie Foxx
4. Lee Lacy, Tony Gwynn
5. Al Rosen
6. Al Oliver
7. Chick Hafey; Bill Terry and Jim Bottomley
8. Cy Seymour
9. Don Mattingly
10. Jack Glasscock in 1890
11. Jackie Robinson
12. Heinie Zimmerman
13. Cleveland; Nap Lajoie, Bobby Avila, and Lou Boudreau
14. Chicago, Cleveland, California; Alex Johnson

23. Highway Robbery

1. Rocky Colavito, Harvey Kuenn
2. Lefty Grove
3. Julian Javier, Dick Groat, Cards
4. Ernie Broglio and Bobby Shantz
5. Orlando Cepeda
6. Steve Carlton
7. Brewers, Ted Simmons, Rollie Fingers, and Pete Vuckovich
8. Willie McGee
9. Jeff Reardon
10. Ken Raffensberger
11. Doc Medich
12. Rogers Hornsby
13. Three Finger Brown
14. Lou Piniella, Seattle Pilots; Amos Otis, Mets; John Mayberry, Astros

24. The Magic Circle

1. Ross Grimsley
2. 1983 White Sox
3. Joaquin Andujar
4. Howie Pollet
5. George Earnshaw
6. Mel Stottlemyre
7. Jim Bagby Sr.
8. Denny McLain, last 30-game winner
9. Sadie McMahon
10. Scott Perry
11. Carl Mays
12. Red Ruffing, Lefty Gomez
13. Bob Porterfield, 1953
14. Pat Malone

25. Jack of All Trades

1. George Kelly, Bill Terry, Frankie Frisch
2. Pete Rose
3. Barry McCormick
4. Tommy Leach
5. Joe Torre
6. Buddy Myer
7. Gil McDougald
8. Ernie Banks
9. Don Buford
10. Dick Allen
11. Jimmy Brown
12. Don Money
13. Pete Runnels
14. Pete Browning

26. Their Niche Is Secure

1. Rogers Hornsby, 1924
2. Mickey Mantle and Ted Williams, 1957
3. Norm Cash
4. Joe Morgan in 1975
5. Lou Gehrig, 1931
6. Chuck Klein, 1930
7. Ted Williams, 1949
8. Steve Carlton, 1980
9. Jim Palmer and Dave Goltz
10. Dwight Gooden, 1985
11. Jack Coombs, 1910
12. Rogers Hornsby and Ty Cobb
13. Walter Johnson
14. Gene Bearden, Boston

27. Great Glovemen

1. Ernie Banks
2. Mike Jorgensen (1973) and Ellis Valentine (1978)
3. Earl Battey
4. Harry Howell
5. Steve O'Neill
6. Willie Kamm
7. Danny Litwhiler, 1942 Phillies
8. Steve Garvey, 1984
9. Pinky Whitney, third base
10. Joe Gerhardt
11. Dal Maxvill
12. Ozzie Smith, 1980

28. Ryan Rousers

1. Frank Robinson and Willie Mays
2. The Alous and the Cruzes
3. Maury and Bump Wills
4. Sandy Koufax
5. Sam McDowell
6. Will Clark
7. Claudell Washington
8. Mel Queen
9. Rickey Henderson
10. Dwight Gooden, set in 1984
11. 1975
12. 1969
13. 1982, Astros
14. 1977
15. Bob Feller

AUGUST

The Sweet Sixteen: Pete Alexander threw 16 shutouts in 1916

29. Home Run Leaders

1. Jimmie Foxx, 1939
2. Dick Allen
3. Tommy Leach, 44 years
4. Roy Sievers, 1957
5. Mike Schmidt, 1974
6. Jack Fournier, 1924
7. Del Ennis
8. Wally Berger and Joe Medwick
9. Jake Stahl
10. Rogers Hornsby, 42 in 1922
11. Darryl Strawberry; Dodgers; Duke Snider in 1956
12. Athletics; Nap Lajoie, Socks Seybold, Tillie Walker, Harry Davis, Jimmie Foxx, Home Run Baker, Gus Zernial
13. Ripper Collins
14. Darrell Evans of the Tigers; Hank Greenberg
15. Tony Conigliaro, 1965 when he was just 20

30. Contact Was Their Middle Name

1. Charlie Hollocher
2. Felix Millan
3. Joe Vosmik
4. Ted Williams and Mel Ott
5. Bill Dickey and Yogi Berra
6. Nellie Fox
7. Lou Boudreau
8. Mickey Cochrane
9. Ted Williams
10. Frankie Frisch
11. Bill Buckner
12. Johnny Mize, 1947
13. Ted Kluszewski
14. Stuffy McInnis
15. Joe DiMaggio

31. Fabled Free Swingers

1. Mickey Mantle and Harmon Killebrew
2. Pete Incaviglia and Juan Samuel; Jose Canseco and Danny Tartabull
3. Tony Perez
4. Rob Deer
5. Dave Nicholson
6. Ron Karkovice
7. Dick Allen
8. Robin Yount
9. Just one, the Angels
10. Andres Galarraga
11. Duke Snider
12. Don Lock and Dave Nicholson
13. Frank Howard

32. Team Teasers

1. Cleveland
2. St. Louis Browns, American Association
3. White Sox, Joe Jackson and Minnie Minoso
4. 1945 Cubs
5. 1952 Tigers
6. Royals
7. Phillies
8. Reds
9. Athletics, 1949–51
10. 1935–36 Boston Braves
11. 1923 Reds
12. 1918–49 Phillies, Pete Alexander and Robin Roberts
13. 1968–80 Orioles, Steve Stone
14. 1968 Cards
15. Brooklyn, 1898–99

33. Shell-Shocked Slingers

1. Paul Foytack, Indians
2. Jim Perry
3. George Caster
4. The Tigers went on strike en masse to protest Ty Cobb's suspension for fighting with a fan; Aloysius Travers
5. Tony Mullane
6. John Coleman
7. Red Ruffing
8. BoBo Newsom, Browns
9. Guy Bush, Cubs
10. Eddie Rommel, A's
11. Bill Carrick
12. Charlie Bicknell
13. Robin Roberts

34. Managerial Musings

1. No, there hasn't been one
2. Johnny Keane in 1964
3. Yankees and Indians; Casey Stengel and Al Lopez
4. Monte Ward
5. Yogi Berra (Lou Boudreau won one the *same* year)
6. Bob Lemon, 1978
7. Bill Terry
8. Gil Hodges
9. Pants Rowland, Ed Barrow
10. Bill Carrigan; 1912, 1915–16
11. Al Lopez
12. Eddie Dyer in 1946
13. Walter Alston
14. Jimmy Dykes, 1934–46 White Sox

35. Their Niche Is Secure

1. Joe Gordon
2. Ernie Banks
3. Eddie Murray
4. Larry Doby
5. Cy Williams; George Crowe; Cliff Johnson
6. Bob Friend
7. Larry Corcoran; Ned Williamson, 1884
8. Fergie Jenkins
9. Bob Gibson
10. Johnny Mize, Cards
11. Jim Rice
12. Jack Clements
13. Sam Thompson
14. Willie McCovey
15. Gavvy Cravath

SEPTEMBER

The Badly Battered Bird: Orioles; Cal Ripken, holder of the record for consecutive innings played with 8,243; Ken Dixon

36. Fabulous Keystone Combos

1. Joe Tinker and Johnny Evers
2. Jackie Robinson and Pee Wee Reese
3. Johnny Evers; Joe Tinker and Rabbit Maranville
4. Travis Jackson; Rogers Hornsby and Frankie Frisch
5. George Davis and Gus Dundon, 1905 White Sox
6. Nap Lajoie and Terry Turner, 1906–07
7. Nellie Fox and Luis Aparicio, 1959
8. Mark Belanger; Davy Johnson and Bobby Grich
9. 1968 Angels; Jim Fregosi and Bobby Knoop
10. Joe Morgan and Dave Concepcion
11. Larry Bowa, Manny Trillo
12. Allan Trammell and Lou Whitaker
13. Ross Barnes and Johnny Peters
14. Bid McPhee and Germany Smith of the Reds
15. Jack Burdock

37. The Magic Circle

1. Joe McGinnity, 1903
2. Bill Hutchinson, 1892
3. Irv Young
4. 1914 Athletics
5. Bob Turley, 1958
6. Bob Feller
7. Dean Chance
8. Howard Ehmke and Sloppy Thurston
9. Fred Goldsmith
10. Johnny Allen in 1937
11. Lefty Grove
12. Lee Richmond
13. Senators (Walter Johnson)
14. Bill Sweeney

38. Silver Sluggers

1. Darryl Strawberry
2. Glenn Wright
3. Wright again
4. Joe Cronin
5. Vern Stephens
6. Al Dark
7. Ernie Banks
8. George Crowe
9. Dave Kingman
10. Harmon Killebrew
11. Phil Bradley
12. Ralph Kiner
13. Stan Musial
14. Larry Parrish, Expos, but credit also for Hector Cruz, Cards

39. Their Niche Is Secure

1. Wade Boggs
2. Stan Musial
3. General Al Crowder
4. Tom Phoebus
5. George McQuillan
6. Reb Russell
7. Maury Wills in 1962 (also broke Cobb's stolen base record that year)
8. Dal Maxvill
9. Dutch McCall
10. Vic Willis and Fergie Jenkins
11. Padres, Joe Lefebvre
12. Cleveland, Brook Jacoby
13. Mel Parnell

40. Minor League Maestros

1. Bill Clymer
2. Joe Bauman
3. Cliff Bolton
4. Ike Boone
5. Larry Gilbert, father of Tookie and Charlie
6. Pancho Herrera
7. Frank Huelsman
8. Tracy "Dick" Barrett
9. Dave Altizer
10. Spider Baum
11. Hooks Iott
12. Rube Robinson
13. Doug Harvey
14. Jack Ogden, brother of Curly

41. They Spelled Relief

1. Greg Olson
2. Jim Konstanty, 1950
3. Warren Spahn
4. Hugh Casey
5. Jesse Barnes, 1921
6. Three Finger Brown, 1908
7. Dizzy Dean, 1936
8. Johnny Sain
9. Mace Brown, 1938 Pirates
10. Roy Face in 1958
11. Mike Marshall, 1974
12. John Hiller
13. They went through the entire season without registering a single save!
14. Walter Johnson
15. Lefty Grove, 1930

42. Hall of Fame Hot Potatoes

1. Joe DiMaggio
2. Pie Traynor
3. Dickie Kerr, victim of the penurious Charlie Comiskey
4. Chief Bender
5. Herman Long
6. Nellie Fox
7. Pete Alexander
8. Harry Stovey
9. 1939–40 Reds, Bill McKechnie and Ernie Lombardi
10. George Kelly
11. Hank Gowdy
12. Virgil "Spud" Davis
13. Frank Killen
14. The A's; Jimmie Foxx, Al Simmons, Lefty Grove, Mickey Cochrane, Ty Cobb, Zach Wheat, and Eddie Collins
15. Jimmy Ryan

OCTOBER

Twin Spoilers: Dave Parker; Bullet Joe Bush; Emil "Irish" Meusel

43. Fall Favorites

1. Joe Wood
2. Jesse Orosco, 1986 NLCS
3. Charlie Silvera and Art Jorgens
4. 1949 Dodgers
5. 1960, Pirates and Yankees
6. 1927 Pirates, Kiki Cuyler and Joe Cronin (Bob Feller sat in 1954)
7. Kip Selbach
8. 1945–46, owing to the many veteran players returning from World War II
9. 1956
10. Buck Herzog, 1912 Giants
11. Tim McCarver
12. Dave Robertson, 1917
13. Irish Meusel
14. Benny Tate
15. Johnny Bench and Thurman Munson

44. Their Niche Is Secure

1. George Bell
2. Walker Cooper
3. Tim Thompson of the 1953 Dodgers
4. Bob Johnson
5. Del Bissonette
6. Boston Braves, Wally Berger
7. Giants, Johnny Mize and Willie Mays
8. Frank Tanana
9. Fergie Jenkins
10. Ivy Wingo
11. Steve Carlton
12. Jim Whitney and Silver King
13. Mel Harder

45. Great Glovemen

1. Nellie Fox
2. Tommy Holmes
3. Sherman Lollar
4. Frank McCormick
5. Lou Boudreau, shortstop
6. Ed Kranepool
7. Del Crandall
8. Hank Majeski
9. Johnny Roseboro
10. Roy Smalley and son
11. Ski Melillo
12. Everett Scott

46. Fall Favorites

1. Denny and Brian Doyle
2. Tommy Henrich, 1949 Yankees
3. Vic Wertz of the 1954 Indians
4. Stan Hack in 1938; Granny Hamner of the 1950 Phils
5. 1923
6. Yankees and Dodgers; 1955 and 1977
7. Jesse Haines and Tommy Thevenow
8. Jack Bentley and Rosy Ryan of the 1924 Giants
9. Luis Tiant in 1975
10. Ken Holtzman in 1974
11. Jack Coombs, A's and Dodgers
12. Jerry Koosman
13. Gene Tenace
14. Willie Aikens in 1980, Dennis Leonard
15. Frankie Frisch

47. Team Teasers

1. 1966 Dodgers
2. 1968 Mets
3. 1915 A's
4. 1949 Red Sox, Ted Williams
5. Cleveland beat Washington
6. Chicago beat Milwaukee
7. Cards beat the Mets
8. Detroit
9. 1938–42 Phillies
10. Braves and Cubs in 1906
11. 1914 Braves, breezed by 10½ games
12. 1902–43 Browns
13. Art Nehf, 1921 Giants
14. Cleveland

48. Their Last Hurrah

1. Bill Bevens,
   Cookie
   Lavagetto
2. Joe Jackson
3. Dave Kingman
4. Nap Lajoie
5. Roberto
   Clemente
6. Sam Rice, Tris
   Speaker

7. Early Wynn
8. Ted Williams
9. Dave Orr
10. Steve Evans
11. Joe Wood
12. Babe Ruth
13. Denny Galehouse
    in 1948
14. Ike Davis
15. Luis Aparicio

49. Fall Favorites

1. Paul Molitor
2. Willie Wilson,
   1980
3. George Pipgras
4. Irv Noren
5. 1965
6. Danny Murtaugh
7. Gabby Hartnett,
   1932 and 1938
8. Dazzy Vance
9. 1890; Brooklyn
   and Louisville;
   Boston of the PL
10. 1910 A's, Eddie
    Plank

11. Mike Torrez, lost
    in the 1978 AL
    East playoff game
12. 1951; Gil
    McDougald
    and Willie Mays;
    Minnie Minoso
    and Chet Nichols
13. 1971; Pirates and
    Orioles
14. 1968, Denny
    McLain and Bob
    Gibson